Cease to Exist

Charles "Tex" Watson
as told to Chaplin Ray Hoekstra

12 A X 7
SANTA MONICA

Originally released as 'Will You Die For Me"?
© 1978 Ray Hoekstra
TX0000016800
©2019 12AX7 Press under assignment V3560D827 & V3617D894
All Rights Reserved
Cover art © Ned Suohevets
info@ceasetoexist.site
v.1002.4

Contents

"Sure Charlie, You Can Kill Me" 1

Behold, He Is In The Desert 11

The Campus Kid 26

The Times, They Are A-Changin' 35

California Dreamin' 46

Gentle Children, With Flowers In Their Hair 55

Family 69

Magical Mystery Tour 79

Watershed: The White Album 91

Happy in Hollywood 105

Revolution/Revelation 112

Piggies 125

You Were Only Waiting for This Moment 138

Helter Skelter I (August 8-9) 149

Helter Skelter II (August 9-10) 165

He's a Runner 176

Inside 185

Jailhouse Religion 195

On Trial 207

Lockup 221

Day 230

To Live is Christ 241

CHARLES "TEX" WATSON

"Sure Charlie, You Can Kill Me"

The point of the long knife pressed against my chest, the blade angled to slide between the ribs, into the heart. All it would take was one quick thrust.

"Will you die for me, Tex? Will you let me kill you?"

It was night, one of those dry, chilly desert nights that can come even while the days are still blistering. We were sitting around a fire.

"Will you let me kill you?"

His voice was soft, very gentle. His eyes seemed to be full of love. I thought of the first time I saw him on the floor of a Pacific Palisades mansion, surrounded by his girls, playing his guitar. "This is Charlie," someone had said, "Charlie Manson." He had looked up with the same dreamy smile he was giving me now over a year since that meeting now, late August 1969 now, with a knife in my side, tripping out in the California desert on the edge of a valley appropriately named Death.

"Let me kill you."

We were camped by the mouth of an abandoned mine shaft in Golar Wash, a rocky scar that slices up into the southern end of the Panamint Mountains. Like Death Valley beyond it, Golar Wash could be some bizarre Martian landscape, or the back side of the moon. At night, with flames reflecting raggedly against the jumble of boulders, it might even pass for hell.

It was a perfect setting, and Charlie knew it; he had an intuitive sense of drama. As he showed later at his trial, he also knew how to play to an audience, and we had an audience that night.

Besides the two of us and Bruce Davis, another Family member, there were three outsiders, guys who'd been with us off and on over the past two weeks, hanging around the edges of things, traveling between Los Angeles and the desert camps.

That day one of them had stolen a dune buggy for us and when we got back to the camp we'd each taken a couple of tabs of acid. They were anxious to please Charlie; they wanted to be part of what we all seemed to have together. I don't think they were ready, though, when he pulled out the knife and turned it slowly back and forth to catch the light of the fire.

"What would you do if I took this knife and started toward you and were going to kill you?" he'd asked them, one by one. They each had answered the same way, grinning nervously, not sure how to take him. They would fight back, they said; they would try to stop him.

"What about you, Tex? Would you die for me? Would you let me kill you?"

I didn't even have to think about it. "Sure, Charlie, you can kill me."

I meant it. Like some mystic, so filled with the love of God that nothing is too great to ask, I was filled with Charlie. He was God to me. A few days before, I'd gone to a pay phone in Olancha — one of the scruffy towns on the highway from Los Angeles — to make a long-distance call to my parents in Texas.

"You've always been wanting me to be religious," I had told my mother. "Well, I've met that Jesus you preach about all the time. I've met him and he's here right now with me in the desert." Charlie was Jesus. He was my messiah, my savior, my soul. It had been true then; it was even truer now. He could ask anything, even my life, and it was his.

And it wouldn't be any great thing, giving him my life, because I knew everything but my physical, animal body was already dead anyway. My ego was dead; anything that asserted *I, me,* or *mine* was dead. My personality had died- now. I was only Charlie, and Charlie was all of me that mattered.

I thought that was beautiful.

"Sure, Charlie, you can kill me."

As I said it, I knew that Charles Denton Watson,—All-American boy, letterman, Scout, Future Farmer of America, twice voted "Campus Kid" at Farmersville High School—*that* Charles Watson was totally dead. I knew it. I had proved it beyond any doubt two and a half weeks before, when in two successive nights I'd killed seven people for Charlie. To do that I'd had to die.

Manson had understood that. He realized that once my own life meant nothing, no one else's life would mean anything either.

The first five killings took place on Cielo Drive in Benedict Canyon, Beverly Hills, just after midnight on Saturday, August 9, 1969. Twenty-four hours later, two more innocent people died on Waverly Drive in the Los Feliz section of Los Angeles near Griffith Park. I had never met any of the victims until a few moments before their deaths. I felt no remorse for the murders, no revulsion at the incredible brutality of the killings. I felt nothing at all.

...not even fear of what might happen if I were caught. Because, like the rest of the Family, I knew a secret: The next day or the day after that (at least sometime very soon), Los Angeles and all the other pig cities would be in flames. It would be the apocalypse, the deserved judgment on the whole sick establishment that hated us and all the other free children, the establishment that had cheated Charlie out of his genius. While the rich piggies lay butchered on their own manicured front lawns, we would have found safety. Charlie would have led us through a secret Devil's Hole into the Bottomless Pit: an underground paradise beneath Death Valley where water from a lake would give everlasting life and you could eat fruit from twelve magical trees: a different one for each month of the year. That would be Charlie's gift to us, his children, his Family.

If anyone back in the Sunday schools I'd attended in Texas had ever mentioned that the Bottomless Pit was one of the biblical names for hell itself, I'd forgotten it.

Even without hope of —the certainty of — escape, there was nothing to be afraid of. In the months before the murders, Charlie had worked with us patiently, lovingly it seemed, until we had touched all our deepest fears, experienced them as completely as we ever could, and gone past them to come out clean on the other side. Charlie had made us see that once you die to your ego, once you strip yourself down to a perfect being — all body. Like some monkey or a coyote free in the wild, not thinking, not willing — once you do that, fear doesn't exist anymore. You've already died, everything except that animal body of yours, so even death can't frighten you. You are free. Free to live, free to die. Free to kill.

The whole world had seen it, the result of that freedom of ours, splattered across their newspapers and magazines and television screens. Half a city had been terrorized, waiting for another night of blood that never came because we had run to the desert.

"Sure, Charlie, you can kill me." Why not? He stared at me with those incredible eyes of his and slowly lowered the knife. He'd made his point. Nobody said anything for a long time.

The slaughter might not have ended with just two nights of murder if my mother hadn't been worried about her son and called a friend of mine in Los Angeles on August 10, the day after the killings at Waverly Drive (actually the day of the murders, since they took place after midnight). She knew nothing about a butchered actress and her friends, or a market owner and his wife ——the deaths weren't creating the mass paranoia and obsessive interest in Texas that they were on the west side of Los Angeles. And the only news that had ever interested her much anyway was when I had been featured on the sports page of the local Farmersville paper. All she knew was that I hadn't contacted my family in over six months.

But I couldn't know that. When my friend called Spahn Movie Ranch where the Family was living, up in the rocky Santa Susana Pass behind Chatsworth (those hills anybody who ever watched old Westerns know like his own backyard), I assumed the F.B.I. or the police had found a fingerprint at Cielo Drive and identified me. I imagined federal agents knocking on my parent's screen door in Copeville, Texas, and telling them their son was a mass murderer. I asked Charlie what to do.

"Call her" he told me. "Find out what's happening."

But I couldn't. Even though I wasn't afraid, somehow I didn't want to know if what I suspected was true. And I didn't want to hear my mother's voice. Several months before, I had reached the place where I could no longer visualize my parents or my sister and brother. It wasn't just that I didn't think about them; I actually could not create in my head an image of what they looked like.

Like all the rest of my life before Charlie, they were dead. I couldn't handle picking up a phone and reconnecting with that past I'd burnt out of my consciousness.

So I lied to Manson, one of the few times I can remember doing so. I claimed I had called home and that my mother had said that F.B.I. men had come to the house looking for me and had told her I was involved in some killings in Los Angeles. As I made up the story for Charlie, I was hoping he'd decide it was time we headed for the desert and started looking for the entrance to the Bottomless Pit. In a few days he did. Now I sometimes wonder how many more nights we might have been sent out with weapons and dark clothing, how many more deaths there might have been if it hadn't been for that telephone call from Texas.

We'd been to the desert before, late in the summer of 1968, checking things out. We knew eventually we'd escape there, when the judgment started to fall on the city. Even though Charlie said that the secret door to the Abyss and the lake was in Death Valley, we'd spent most of our time just west of the Valley itself, over the Panamint Mountains a few miles south of the desert town of Ballarat.

Charlie was especially attracted to two isolated ranches at the top of Golar Wash -- Myers and Barker. The Wash —even by day, without LSD and a knife in your ribs— was hellish, unbelievably rugged. It could take a good half a day to work your way up on foot, and even the toughest jeep would have a hard time against the boulders and narrow turns. The ranches themselves were about a quarter of a mile apart. Myers Ranch came first and was in very bad condition, rundown and vandalized, but Barker Ranch had a solid little stone ranch house and a swimming pool, even sheets on the beds. Later the place would be described as derelict and dilapidated, but we had less exacting standards it was part of being natural and free from the uptight programming our parents had laid on us.

Charlie liked Barker Ranch so much he even contacted Arlene Barker to get her permission for him and a "few" of his friends to camp there. She was living at another house down in Panamint Valley and I don't think she had any idea how many of us there were or how long Charlie was planning to need the place. People who live in a place like Death Valley are pretty tolerant, and Charlie was always good at a con; it was something I think he'd learned in prison. He laid a line on Mrs. Barker that he was the manager for the Beach Boys rock group and, to prove it, gave her the gold record they had received for selling a million copies of *The Beach Boys Today* album. Dennis Wilson —a member of the group who accidentally became my link with Manson— had given it to Charlie when some of Manson's girls were living in Wilson's mansion on Sunset Boulevard. Whether she bought the story or not, Mrs. Barker said we could use the place.

But now, strangely, Charlie didn't send me to Barker or Myers. Instead, he decided I should stay at a small ranch outside of Olancha, twenty miles across the Panamint Valley from Golar Wash, at the base of the Sierra Nevadas. The place belonged to a young dude who fancied himself a cowboy and had been with us on and off at Spahn Ranch for several weeks. Charlie told me to go there, at least for a while, so the cowboy and I loaded up the Family truck with some supplies and a dune buggy I'd been working on and headed out for Olancha with Juan Flynn, one of the ranch hands at Spahn. Juan was from Panama and had never become part of the inner circle of the Family, but he hung around with us a lot, even after Charlie threatened to kill him several times.

About two miles down the highway toward the desert we were pulled over by a county sheriff's car. My first rush of adrenaline subsided when it became clear they had nothing more on their minds than a search of the truck for stolen property. When they found out we were from Spahn Ranch, several other cars were called in. Even though the Manson Family was not as notorious then as we soon would be, local law enforcement in Chatsworth was aware that quite a congregation of hippie types was living up at the old movie ranch in the pass, and there were suspicions we weren't paying for all the vehicles and spare parts that kept appearing in the gullies and washes behind the rundown sets and stables.

When the officers questioned me, I told them my name was Charles Montgomery. It was not an alias I pulled out of the air. Montgomery was my mother's maiden name. My second cousin, Tom Montgomery, was the sheriff of

Collin County, Texas, and four months later he would receive a call from the Los Angeles County District Attorney's office telling him I was wanted for murder. I suppose I thought it was a pretty good joke, using my pig cousin's name to fool pigs. The real irony of the situation didn't come home to me until much later. Within three days of the grotesque murders that were at that very moment being spread across the consciousness of America, law enforcement officers had the primary culprit in custody and they let him go. They didn't even discover the two stolen Volkswagen motors we had stashed in the back of the truck!

Behold, He Is In The Desert

The "ranch" turned out to be nothing but an uninhabitable old shack a few hundred yards down the road from Olancha. An irrigation ditch ran along one side of the place, and before we'd finished unloading the truck I'd decided that camping down there would be better than trying to clean up the house.

As I watched the cowboy and Juan drive off-back to Spahn and Charlie and all the others—I suddenly realized that for the first time since the weekend and the blood, I was completely alone. I could see Olancha squatting down the road, not much more than a truck stop, shimmering in the heat waves and dust, but it was full of strangers. Strangers must be hostile - because they weren't Family. Olancha had nothing for me. In every other direction all you could see was desert, emptiness, and heat rimmed with naked hills. I was by myself —no Family, no Charlie, no girls to look after me or make love to me— just my racing brain for company.

I had an urge to stretch out under that searing desert sun and just roast out of me every thought, every sensation. But my mind wouldn't stop flying, speeding back over those two nights and the days before them, the days ahead, maybe tomorrow, maybe tonight, when Helter Skelter would come roaring down on the world. I should start organizing the supplies; I should start looking for the Bottomless Pit; I should move around; I should catch up with time rushing like wind past my ears. My bombed-out brain was whipping around inside my skull and I couldn't stop it; even that huge sun couldn't stop it, slow it down, and give me rest.

I spent most of the next day watching, waiting like an animal that knows the hunt's on. Then the truck appeared again. This time the driver was one of Charlie's ex-convict friends who had been wandering in and out of the fringes of the Family for a couple of months. He was never much interested in Helter Skelter or the end of the world; armed robbery was good enough for him. But the Family provided him a base of operations and available women, and Manson and he had been friends in prison; so he spent time with us and did things for Charlie.

He brought two of the youngest Family members with him, which made me think that either Charlie was taking my lie about the F.B.I. pretty seriously, or he had some other reason for expecting things to start coming down. He seemed to be getting the underage people out of Spahn Ranch and, with them, the legal hassles they could cause if there were a raid. With the two kids —a boy and a girl— he brought some food and a little money. Once again the truck rolled out for Spahn. Now I had company.

I don't remember the boy's name but the girl was Dianne Lake; we used to call her "Snake." She was one of the saddest members of the Family; so young, only thirteen when she joined (with her parents' okay, as Manson liked to brag), and Charlie used to hit her and pull her hair a lot. Once he whipped her with an electric cord, but she still stayed around and loved him. She was nearly sixteen by now, quiet, always sort of apologetic in the way she acted.

The three of us camped out down by the irrigation ditch, swimming naked, using some trees on the other side of the house for a bathroom, not saying much. When Dianne and I went into Olancha to buy more food, I bought a newspaper to check out news about the murders. From what I could tell, the police didn't know anything that would tie the Family to the deaths, at least anything they were talking about, so I relaxed a little about the call from my mother. But my head wouldn't let go of it. While I had been with Charlie, the Family all around me, things had seemed to make a certain kind of sense, but now, stuck out in the desert with these two kids, I got more and more confused. I even began to feel fear again, the kind of nameless fear I'd known as a child when I thought my parents might catch me in some lie, a fear that makes you feel like you have to do something quick to fix things before you get caught.

But I didn't know what to do. How could this be fixed? That night I felt so wound up inside that I started talking to Dianne and finally admitted to her that I was the one who'd stabbed that beautiful blond actress, stabbed her again and again, over and over, stabbed her because

Charlie told me to. Dianne got even quieter after that, but she didn't try to run.

I was so mixed up that the next afternoon I just suddenly left the two of them at our camp by the ditch and walked into Olancha and hitched a ride back to Los Angeles with one of the truckers. He dropped me off at La Cienega about eight o'clock that night. As I hitched up La Cienega toward the Hollywood Hills and Sunset Strip, I noticed headlines on some cheap newspapers that were trying to claim the Beverly Hills murders had been the result of a black-magic sex orgy or a drug bum or something wild the victims had been doing. Sticking out my thumb, I thought how all those cars going by were full of people who wondered who did it and why it was done. And I knew-and it was so bizarre that they wouldn't begin to believe me if I tried to tell them, tried to explain that seven people were brutally murdered so the world as we know it could begin to burn and Manson —Jesus Christ— could lead his children to safety inside the Earth.

On my way up into the Strip area I stopped to look into the windows of a wig shop where I'd worked when I first came to Los Angeles from Texas two years before. I'd expected a lot back then: a whole new life as a whole new person, never stuck in the Texas back country again. Now here I was, that new person; dirty, itchy, spaced out, face pressed against the glass of the dark shop with the name of a movie star going around in my head: Sharon Tate. I'd never seen one of her films, never really heard of her or seen her photograph. All I knew of her was as a terrified woman begging to be allowed to have her child before we killed her.

I didn't know why I'd come down to Los Angeles or where I was headed. I stopped by an old girlfriend's house but no one was home. I wandered some on Sunset Strip. It had been like another world when I came to Los Angeles in 1967: hippies and psychedelic shops and people "turning on" on the sidewalk. There weren't the crowds anymore; in two years the shops were already starting to look seedier. I hitched over Laurel Canyon into the Valley. I thought of going up to Spahn. I wanted to see Charlie, at least a part of me did. But I also wanted to run away from Charlie. I had, once before, but he'd drawn me back. I thought about calling my parents and asking for the money to come home to Texas, but I decided the first place the police would look for me would be home with my folks. And Charlie had put me in charge of those two kids up in Olancha. He wouldn't like it if I ran away. And as much as I might want to run, where was there to run to? I got on an entrance ramp of the San Diego Freeway and by the next morning had hitched my way back to Olancha. I don't think Dianne ever asked me where I'd been.

Although we didn't find out about it for several days, on Saturday morning, August 16, the morning I got back from my sixteen-hour circle to Los Angeles and back, sheriff's deputies raided Spahn Ranch, arresting Charlie and all the rest of the Family on suspicion of grand theft auto. For the second time within a week of the murders, police had the killers everybody was talking about in custody (at least some of them) and for the second time they released them, this time after a couple of days in jail. The warrant on which the arrest was made had been misdated.

About four days after I got back, Dianne was picked up by the deputy sheriff from Independence while she was in Olancha buying food. Independence was the closest town with law enforcement, about thirty miles farther up the highway from our truck stop. As a lot of the Family did at one time or another, Dianne had some sort of skin disease and when she told the deputy she was nineteen and just hitchhiking through, he took her home and his wife fed her and gave her a salve for her skin. When he brought her back to Olancha she sneaked back to the camp.

The next afternoon, the same deputy drove up outside our shack, responding to a complaint by some of the local people who'd seen us swimming nude in the irrigation ditch. I was asleep on an old cot in the shade behind the house and my heart started pounding when I woke up and saw the car and the lawman talking to Dianne and the boy. My first impulse was to run, so I started off into the trees; but it seemed pointless, so I came back out and sauntered up to the car, claiming I had just been relieving myself in the woods. Putting on my heaviest Texas drawl, I told him my name was Charles Montgomery and gave him my actual age and date of birth. The deputy made out a field report on me and took in Dianne and the boy. We never saw the boy again. I presume he was sent back to his parents, but

Dianne was back at camp a few hours later. In the next few days five other girls from the Family came up from Spahn and the deputy sheriff ended up chauffeuring them back out to our camp every time they'd hitch into Olancha. I think he did it partly out of kindness and partly out of suspicion. Whatever the reasons, I wasn't comfortable having police around so much, so I called Charlie and he decided it was time everybody should move up to the two ranches in Golar Wash. It was time to start looking for the entrance to the Bottomless Pit.

The week or so that followed was taken up by a confused series of trips back and forth between Spahn and the desert, back-breaking hauls of dune buggies and supplies up the rock-strewn Wash, frantic stashing of guns and vehicle parts in scattered gullies and ravines, and setting up camp at Myers Ranch. We made dozens of day-long trips up the Wash in the blazing August sun, dragging up everything the Family owned on our backs. A big school bus that we'd had for over a year was driven in from the Las Vegas side and parked at Barker Ranch. It was preparation for war, the final war. If we didn't find the entrance to our underground haven in time, we'd be ready for the black man once he came after us; we'd fight him off until that moment when the sand would swallow us up. Charlie seemed to have more power in him than ever before. He moved faster; you could almost see the energy streaming out of him, like rainbow waves on one of those black-light posters we'd kept at Spahn Ranch. We would be ready; he would see to that. So we followed his orders, we pushed ourselves to dropping, we fortified Myers Ranch and waited for it to begin.

We weren't alone at the ranch. Along with swarms of black bats that we were convinced came from the Abyss we were searching for, we had human company. A man named Paul Crockett was living in a cabin near Myers Ranch and he had two younger men with him who had belonged to the Family the year before, when we first came up to the desert. Charlie had sent them back up in March to stake our claim on the ranches, and somehow they'd gotten in with Crockett; he had begun deprogramming them from Manson's control to a Scientology trip he was on that was similar to Charlie's in some of its terminology and concepts, but not as dangerous. Crockett did not believe anything he heard about Helter Skelter or lakes under the desert.

Manson had never had any competition within the Family and he didn't quite know what to do with this forty-five-year-old man, especially the fact that he had managed to turn two Family members against him. Charlie had been careful never to tell us the sources of any of his ideas (except for the Bible and the Beatles). Most of us just assumed they were wisdom he had come to on his own. Now here was someone who could argue with Charlie on his own terms, toss around the same language and ideas, but come up at a different place with them. For a while Charlie talked about killing him. Finally the two of them sat down for a three-day marathon conversation and argument. When it was over they had established a kind of wary truce, though I know

Crockett was afraid Manson would try to murder him, up until the time he was arrested. Even though he gave us help hauling things up from the bottom of Golar Wash to the ranch, he slept with a shotgun by his side at night. What probably saved his life was a series of little coincidences that convinced Charlie he had power, too -— spiritual power, energy, like Manson himself had.

Crockett wasn't the only one who was threatened with death, though as far as I know no one was actually killed in the desert while I was there, despite what some people claimed later. Another one of Charlie's old prison buddies was helping move things up from Spahn in his four-wheel-drive truck, and when Manson found out he was also stealing from us he vowed to cut him up if he came back again. He never did.

Charlie seemed on edge, nervous a lot of the time, hyper. One day he'd be deciding we should live at Myers Ranch, then the next we'd suddenly pack up and move to Barker, then he'd change his mind and order us to camp outside to keep watch for the blacks and the pigs. Meanwhile, Family women were coming and going from Spahn, bringing back food and visitors— it seemed like every day there were different people, different plans.

Nights were heaviest. We'd take acid, and Charlie would get into really strong programming —that is, destroying whatever ego we might have left in us. Sometimes he'd lunge at me and scream that because of the murders, I had the same thing coming to me. I'd taken on the karma of those deaths, the violence, and it would come back to me like a boomerang.

"Do you feel guilty for what you did?" he'd scream three or four times.

"No," I'd say. "I don't feel guilty; I don't feel anything."

"Well, I want you to feel guilty about it. Feel guilty! Feel guilty! Feel guilty!"

"I will if that's what you want, Charlie." But I didn't. I couldn't.

Suddenly he'd laugh and go on to something else. The stars would be spread out in the black sky above us and he'd be dancing around the fire, dancing into our heads, threatening to kill anyone who tried to leave. We belonged together, we were a Family, and anyone who broke the bond would have his throat cut.

In the middle of all this Charlie decided we needed more dune buggies. Eventually he planned for each of the men to have one, a kind of army of dune buggies to patrol the desert like German Field Marshal Rommel and the Afrika Korps during the Second World War. I never quite understood how this fit in with our escaping into the Bottomless Pit, except that it began to look as if the Abyss would be harder to find than we'd first thought. In the meantime we might have to fight off an enemy that sometimes consisted of black revolutionaries bringing on Helter Skelter and sometimes pigs, establishment cops. At night we kept lookout in the hills, flying over the sand and back roads like wild people in our dune buggies —renegade Indians with buckskin and knives.

Charlie sent Bruce Davis and me to Los Angeles with three newcomers who had been drifting in and out of the Family over the past weeks. Our assignment was to steal transportation. We did. One of the new boys took a brand-new dune buggy off the lot in Long Beach for a "test drive" and drove it all the way up to Golar Wash without looking back; I hot-wired a red Toyota jeep on the street. When we got back that night, camp had been moved again. Now Charlie had a base set up for himself and a few others behind the entrance to the Lotus Mine shaft in the Wash. He'd been out all day chasing two of the girls who had run away and he was "wired," throwing out energy. We all dropped acid, and just before it started to "come on," Charlie pulled out his knife slowly, turning it in the firelight. You know the rest . . . .

Even though I was willing to die for Charlie, I was getting tired of breaking my back for him. It seemed as if every day there was less chance of finding the Pit, no matter how much we drove around over the desert, no matter how many abandoned mine shafts we crawled through. We were short of food, we were allowed only one cup of water per day and, worst of all, the drugs were running out. For the first time I began to wonder, somewhere in the back of my head, if everything Charlie said was sure to come true after all.

Charlie decided he wanted to own Myers Ranch so he sent Catherine Gillies —the one we called "Capistrano"— to Fresno to murder her grandmother who happened to own it. She was also supposed to kill any other members of her family who might be in line to claim title. One of the newer boys went with her and I never found out exactly what went wrong. It was something to do with a flat tire and their getting caught trying to pose as man and wife. It may have boiled down to the fact that they weren't as dead as some of the rest of us were - but the grandmother survived and they didn't come back. I could understand their staying away once they'd failed on one of Charlie's orders. You didn't disappoint him, no matter what it took. I'd proved that. But even though they didn't come back, they didn't turn him in, either. You might not be able to face "God," but he was still God-Charlie and you respected him.

By this time I would assume that at least half of the Family knew something about our involvement in the murders in Los Angeles. And we had reason to believe there would be more killings to come. Charlie was threatening first this outsider then that one. He had given each of the girls her own Buck knife and had them practicing how to slit pigs' throats —pull back the heads by the hair and slice from ear to ear. The girl he used as a model for this demonstration was so scared she tried to run away, but he pulled a knife on her and made her take the last of the acid. The vibrations weren't what they had been before; it was as if the Satan who Charlie sometimes claimed to be was striking out at even the Family itself.

At first it was a kind of trip, not eating, drying up under the desert sun. After all the acid we had taken, we became very aware of our bodies, as if we could see into and under the skin. Charlie said that it was the pigs who stuffed themselves; we should cut down on our food and water and sweat the poisons out. We could see that happening, the things that weren't "us" boiling to the surface of our skin and dripping away. But when he began feeding what little food we had left to some burros at Barker Ranch, I started wondering if he knew what he was doing.

Between looking for hiding places and looking for the tunnel that would lead us under the desert to our home, we covered most of Death Valley during September. We knew that sheriffs and National Park rangers were watching us and that added to our paranoia. One night we found that a road we had been using had been torn up by a skip loader. A few nights later we found the offending machine and poured gasoline over it and set it on fire. You could see the blaze for miles.

People are bound to ask at some point if Manson actually believed we would find the Bottomless Pit — or if it was a delusion he merely fostered among his followers. I will never know for certain, but I'm convinced he believed it as much as we did. He was absolutely sure he was Jesus Christ — it had been revealed to him three years before on an LSD trip in San Francisco — so why shouldn't he lead us first into the Pit and then back out of it to rule the world? He shared the madness he created in us; he was finally its most ardent disciple.

Late in September, having failed to "inherit" Myers Ranch through murder, Charlie went to Arlene Barker again and offered to buy her ranch. He gave her a new line — he was no longer working with the Beach Boys; now he was in the film business and wanted to buy the ranch for movie locations. She asked for cash and that ended it.

Day after day the search continued and still we found nothing. Since our midnight bonfire with the skip loader, attention from the authorities had increased and on September 29 Ranger Dick Powell and California Highway Patrolman James Pursell surprised some of the girls and me in one of the gullies behind Barker. I ran off naked before they could talk to me. While they were there the two officers took parts out of the engine of the Toyota jeep I'd hot-wired the month before, but it still ran and as soon as they were gone we drove off into one of the canyons nearby and covered it with camouflage.

All the next day, from our lookout posts in the hills, we watched the National Park rangers driving back and forth like ants over the desert roads, looking for us. After it got dark, Charlie and I drove all night by the light of the moon, surveying his desert kingdom. He was very quiet, wound up like a spring. When we got back to Myers Ranch early the next morning, he handed me a double-barreled shotgun that had been stolen from one of the girls' parents before we left Los Angeles.

"Go up into the attic there," he said to me, pointing to a place where the attic extended out over the porch of the ranch house with gaping holes between the boards. "Go up there with this and wait. When those two rangers come, kill them."

He drove off and I climbed into the hot, dusty attic to wait.

The Campus Kid

When I woke up in the attic at Myers Ranch the next morning, early on the morning of October 2, a shotgun was cradled in my arms. I knew why. I was waiting to kill two National Park rangers when they came looking for the arsonists who had burned their earthmover. Charlie had told me to kill them, just as he had told me to kill before.

I looked down at the gun and knew, just as certainly as I knew what he had told me, that I was not going to use it. I was not going to kill again for Charles Manson.

I'll never be sure exactly why I was able to say no then, when for the past eight months it had always been 'yes' for Charlie. I think it had something to do with being without drugs for two or three weeks. Suddenly I didn't believe we were ever going to find the secret hole into the Pit; suddenly I knew the world was not going to end; suddenly I was tired and hungry; suddenly I didn't care what Charlie had told me to do —all I knew was that I would not kill anyone. Not again.

I tossed down the gun and went downstairs as fast as I could. Sorting through a pile of clothes we had all shared, I picked out the best shirt and pants I could find and ran out to a Dodge power wagon we had parked behind the house. Now it seemed inevitable that the rangers would be there at any moment, and my hands shook as I started the wagon and tore off down the Wash. Golar Wash was never meant for driving, much less at the speeds I was taking it, but I knew I had to get away before Charlie or the rangers or anyone else found me and stopped me. I knew if I could make it to Ballarat, the town a few miles up from the mouth of the Wash, I could hitch a ride back into Los Angeles. I had to make it to Ballarat.

I finally roared out of the Wash onto the unpaved road toward town. About three quarters of the way there I realized I was running out of gas. I turned off the road and started out across the salt flats —a shortcut across an air-force testing ground to the road to Trona, eighteen miles or so to the southwest. Halfway across the flats the wagon died, bogged down in the salt and out of gas. I jumped out and started walking, leaving the door hanging open behind me. The sun beat down, dazzling up from the white salt all around. Suddenly there was an enormous roaring, like the Apocalypse I'd been waiting for so long. I threw myself flat on the ground just as an air-force jet flew over me, hugging the flats so close I was sure it would hit me. The sound waves rolled off into the empty desert and I got up and walked to the highway down to Trona where an old prospector picked me up in his jeep.

It's a long ride from the desert to Los Angeles, but I made it in one ride that took me to San Bernardino. I called my parents and told them I wanted to come home. When the money arrived an hour later at Western Union, I went to a store and bought a pair of Levi's, a coat, and new shoes. It wasn't enough —I was shaggy and filthy, with my hair full of sand and salt. I changed clothes behind a building and gulped down a Big Mac. It was the first meat I'd had in months and I thought I was going to throw up.

A helicopter took me from the San Bernardino airport to Los Angeles International and while I was waiting for my flight to Texas I had my hair cut and washed. When my sister and her husband picked me up at Love Field in Dallas at five o'clock the next morning, the first thing they said was that my Los Angeles International haircut was still too long for Texas. As soon as the barbershops opened they took me in for another trim, before my parents saw me. "And this time make him look like a boy." I was home. Texas. Copeville —a few white frame buildings scattered on either side of the railroad; my father's store and gas pumps; my mother in her kitchen with the picture of the Last Supper over the dinner table. From where I'd come it was as far away as the moon, and just as unreal.

The Copeville I grew up in was like a lot of small Texas towns in the fifties, only smaller. Early in the century it had boasted a whole main street, even one brick building, but by the time I was born the years and the Great Depression had wiped out most of that. Now the white wooden buildings were separated by vacant lots scattered with rusting junk. From beside the gas pumps out in front of my father's store you could see nearly all there was left of Copeville —peeling white on gray, with green weeds sprouting up in the open spaces in the spring.

My folks were married during the Depression and spent several years living off a small garden and a few animals until they scraped together enough capital to buy one of Copeville's stores, the whole place about the size of a single-car garage. It had one gas pump in front-a real pump that lived up to its name; you pumped the gas by hand. Over the years they built their house, enlarged the store, added new automatic pumps, and had three children who they were determined would have the chances they never did. They worked hard; they believed in a God who rewarded hard work and simple values. They believed in an America that was always right and would never change — not in any way that couldn't be made right by an appeal to the way "decent" folks had always done things.

I was born on December 2, 1945, exactly two months after V-J Day. America was the moral champion of the world. And it would always be that way. We would always fight on the side of right and justice, and the wars we fought we would win. It wasn't for nothing that Eisenhower added "under God" to the flag salute shortly after I started school.

God was very much a part of my world. He was the One you talked to every Sunday at the Copeville Methodist Church. He was the One who had long blond hair and a beard (like no other man you ever saw) and wore a white robe and sat under palm trees with children on his knees in the Sunday-school calendars. Next to my stuffed panda bear and my older brother, God was probably one of my favorite people. When I prayed as "I lay me down to sleep," that the Lord would keep me, the Lord was a hazy mix of that long-haired, bearded man in the Sunday-school pictures, my mother, and Santa Claus.

According to church records, I received Christ as my personal Savior in August 1958 and was baptized and received into church membership. What I remember most vividly was being told in class one Sunday morning that two other kids and I had reached the age at which we would join the church and be sprinkled. For some reason I didn't like the sound of that so I ran all the way home and hid under the covers, even though I was twelve years old. I finally went through with it, to please my parents and because it was what you did when you turned twelve. I wasn't even conscious of any deception in the act. Being in church and being a Christian were just part of what it meant to be a young American boy, a Scout, a good citizen, and a Future Farmer of America. Religion was important, especially for women and old people, but the only folks who got carried away with it were some blacks and poor white trash that we called "Holy Rollers." I never saw a "Holy Roller" in the flesh, but I knew that they were almost as "bad" as the Catholics.

As I got older, I was involved in activities at church, even led devotions for the youth group and gave talks for Sunday-night evangelistic services. Inside, I was beginning to feel as if God and my mother had one more thing in common —they both wanted to hold me down, keep me from doing the things I wanted to. They both said, "No!" and "Bad!" to some of the urges I was starting to feel, especially about girls. But Mom wasn't very hard to fool, so I supposed God wouldn't be either.

My childhood was very happy. There was an older brother with whom I only started to feel I had to compete as I got into high school. There was an older sister who raised me almost as much as my mother. There was a big collie dog and there were my projects. Even before I started school I began making things with my hands —little cars, models, toys. And from the time I was six I helped my father in the store and worked on the onion harvest each year.

After my arrest, the media had a field day comparing Copeville's Charles Watson —honor student, track star (my record in high hurdles still stands), Yell Leader, the boy next door with the crew cut and the prize-winning calf —to the doped-up killer who grinned stupidly out of *Life* magazine with glazed eyes. "If it can happen to an all-American boy like this," the articles and picture spreads seemed to be asking, "what about your own children?"

I went to school in Farmersville, a few miles up the road from Copeville. It was home of the "Fighting Farmers" and had also been the home of Audie Murphy. Some people thought I might be the next son of Farmersville to bring fame and pride to that dusty little community.

When I was only ten a local reporter commented in print on my industry in gathering and selling crawdads to fishermen on a nearby lake. Three times during my years in high school I was chosen "Campus Kid" by the Hi Life school newspaper staff. They noted that I was active in everything from the school band to the yearbook to the paper itself to drama. And there was sports.

My brother had been a football hero at Farmersville High before me, and I very quickly realized I had a legend to live up to. I was determined to better it. In eighth grade I entered my first track meet and walked away with five first-place blue ribbons. They were not the last. My mother kept them all in an old tie box and as the semesters went by, meet after meet, the box started getting stuffed. I wasn't content with just track — I went out for basketball and lettered in football, left halfback. I played on district teams, was voted honorable mention, all district. I won more ribbons and my mother started collecting clippings from the sports pages of the local papers.

In my junior year I became co-sports editor of Hi Life with my buddy Tommy Caraway. Although we'd have been embarrassed by the word at the time, I really loved Tommy. We hung around together, worked on the sports section of the yearbook, talked about our futures, what we wanted out of life. It seemed as if what we mainly wanted at that point was women. We'd tool around the country roads in a 1956 Mercury two-door hardtop I'd bought from my brother-in-law and sneak beer and water-ski in the hot summer months. We thought we'd live forever.

I was determined to go to college. I worked summers and afternoons in an onion-packing plant, saving money, and in between school and work I found time to rebuild cars (a skill of mine Manson would find useful a few years later) and make a pool table from scratch, even time to get to know a particular girl who gossip had it was "easy."

I think one reason the sexual freedom I found later in California, especially in the Family, seemed so liberating at the time was the fact that sex was never discussed much in my family —somehow it seemed forbidden, secret, dirty. Growing up in the country, you couldn't help discovering how things worked, and as strange changes started happening in your body there were always other, wiser boys who could tell you what "it" was like and how to get it, even if you didn't talk about it at home. There were the usual whispered conversations in locker rooms and on overnight visits, the Playboy centerfolds sneaked out of an older, college-age brother's room and shared among the team, the campus rumors about which girls would and which wouldn't. In that day before the Pill, there was always the chance of pregnancy, and you knew once that happened it was a church wedding and baby pictures seven months later. The problem was that the girls you'd want to marry didn't, and the girls that did weren't the kind of girls you took home to meet your folks for Sunday dinner.

It's probably hard for kids growing up today to understand, but the early sixties, at least in Texas, were still times when stealing a quick caress on top of some high-school junior's bra in the backseat of a buddy's car seemed unbelievably exciting and forbidden and could provide fantasy material for weeks. And no matter how bad my mother or the church might say it was, I knew what I wanted and I found a girl who would give it to me. The only problem was the fact that her reputation had spread beyond the locker room. My parents told me not to see her anymore. That didn't stop me.—we just met in secret for those clumsy encounters. If I felt any guilt at all, it just added to the excitement. I told myself that my parents just didn't understand what it was like to be sixteen . . . . Just like — good Methodists that they were —they made a big fuss about beer, but once I tried it I found out you didn't get roaring drunk on your first sip.

My parents' world of church and God and rules wasn't what I wanted. I was a success, I could handle my life without them or that pale-faced Jesus in the church magazines. I started to think about getting out, finding a larger, more exciting world where everybody didn't know you and every false step wouldn't get reported and discussed within twenty-four hours behind the counter of my father's store.

The Times, They Are A-Changin'

Denton, Texas, was only fifty miles from Copeville, but it meant being on my own. North Texas State University was attended mainly by people with country Texas backgrounds a lot like mine, but it was away from home.

It was September, 1964, and I was going to be Joe College. My parents expected great things from me — after all, hadn't I graduated from Farmersville High with honors? I expected freedom.

In other places around the country, students were taking off in new directions that would not only lead a whole generation to a radical break from the comfortable fifties' womb we'd all grown up in, but would destroy that world forever. We didn't know or care about all that in Denton. For us, college still meant fraternities and hazing and driving down to Dallas with a fake I.D. that got you into German beer halls where you drank out of pottery steins and sang along with a polka band.

The only drug anybody knew much about was Dexedrine, brought over the border from Mexico to keep you awake for finals cramming. It wasn't until my junior year that dope was ever even talked about. By then rumor had it that one of the guys was smoking marijuana in his room sometimes, but it was not considered cool, and at N.T.S.U. there was nothing more important than being cool.

Cool meant parties and beer and women —the same as high school but more of each. Cool was dressing well. I started buying new clothes, wide ties and button-down shirts and a camel's hair blazer with metal buttons. I combed down the crew cut and let it grow a little —the barber called it the Ivy League look.

We weren't that interested in classes (my grades soon showed it), and if anybody ever talked about politics he meant civics lectures on a bicameral legislative branch, not people in the streets. We were proud to be Americans — if we thought about it. We would have undoubtedly said communism was bad, if anybody bothered to ask us — communists wanted to bury us. The world outside was simple; Lyndon Johnson was "a good ol' boy" from Texas and nobody really knew much about some kind of military assistance we were giving over in Southeast Asia.

It was a time when you thought of the Golden Gate, not the Haight, when somebody mentioned San Francisco. If we'd have seen a man with hair to his shoulders we'd have called him a "pansy," not a "hippie," and a beard was something you let grow over vacation on a dare, then shaved off.

After living for eighteen years in the same white frame house in Copeville, I suppose I felt pretty mature moving into a student residence hall near the campus. I woke up the first morning with the exhilarating realization that I could do whatever I wanted and nobody would care.

My roommate was a junior transfer from Texas State in Austin, and from the very beginning I got in with a group older than I was. They knew how to dress, where to take a woman, and had a reputation for being a little wild. I was impressed. I also learned fast. When frat rushes started during second semester, there was no question where I'd end up. I'd already been careening around campus in Pi Kappa Alpha's old fire truck with the rest of the boys for several months.

Part of the fraternity initiation was a scavenger hunt. It was more than a game; your being pledged depended on getting every item on the list. And PKA tradition made it clear that there was more than one acceptable way to pick up what you needed. My partner and I had to find, among other things, four typewriters. Through the beer-soaked fog that traditionally surrounded events like this, I remembered the typing class at Farmersville High School, with row on row of battered Royals. Getting them was easy — break the glass, open the door, giggle a lot, and shush each other boozily. It seemed extremely funny. The next day, with a throbbing hangover, four typewriters, and the certainty of being caught, it seemed extremely stupid.

Rather than have them find out from someone else, I went to my parents myself. They took it hard, and as we drove into McKinney, the county seat, to talk to a lawyer, I fumed to myself that they couldn't have been any more upset if I'd committed murder.

The lawyer was Roland Boyd, a Texas gentleman of the old school, whose family had been close to my mother's people for several generations. Because I turned myself and the typewriters in, or — possibly — because Roland's son Bill was county district attorney at the time, I was not even booked. But to be sure I didn't get the wrong impression, Mr. Boyd took me into his paneled conference room for a stern talk about staying out of trouble in the future. I assured him I would. As he sat talking to me about my fine high-school record and my parents' feelings, neither of us could possibly anticipate those same parents sitting in that same room four years later, asking him and his son to represent me on a charge of murder.

Back among the Pikes (our campus nickname), it started to seem a little funny again. It was, after all, part of our reputation to be riding just over the edge of the law occasionally. A year later, when a beer bottle tossed drunkenly out of a car destroyed a boy's eye, that reputation took on a darker tone. Even though I wasn't involved, my minister in Copeville took the opportunity to write me a long letter of concern. His major point was the assurance that he did not condemn the whole house through guilt by association, but what I noticed most was his comment that incidents like this were one reason the Methodist church opposed drinking. The rules again ... I wasn't interested in what he had to say about character and moral stamina. I wasn't interested in the counsel and prayers he offered. I was too busy having fun.

Life was a succession of parties, interrupted by a minimal amount of studying. Except for a fraternity track meet where I ran the high hurdles, I didn't get involved in sports at college; they took too much time and effort. Sitting over drinks at Lou Ann's in Dallas, or making a run to our local college tavern for beer, I'd think that this was what life was all about: having good times with your buddies. Swing-dancing to the Five Americans, or persuading a girl I'd still respect her, I'd think back to my last few years at home and wonder how I'd survived all my parents' rules and old-fashioned attitudes. Even then—fifty miles away with my own apartment and a new 1966 Coronet 500 and a boat and all the friends I could want—even then they were still in the background, checking up on me, asking about the girls I saw and what they were doing at my apartment so much, asking why my grades weren't what they'd been in high school, urging me to start going to church again. It was love that made them concerned, but at the time all I could sense was oppression. Even away from Copeville, the world I'd grown up in was stifling me, putting limits on my freedom. I began to think maybe I needed to get even farther away.

By the time I started my junior year, I even had an idea what "farther away" would be like: California. My generation wasn't the first to get hooked on the special, somehow magical appeal of the Coast. There had been the perfect climate, the orange trees, then Hollywood and the chance to become a film star (our democracy's answer to royalty). In the sixties, California meant beaches and surfing and endless summers. When I was still at home, my brother had collected almost every album the Beach Boys made and, although I wasn't that into music, I heard them from behind his door, singing about "California Girls" in a way that made Texas women seem a little less exciting than they had before, singing about the surfing that was some kind of golden fantasy for us, but a way of life in California. I could never have imagined that one day one of those superstars would take me into his home and introduce me to an aspiring rock singer named Charlie Manson.

Even if I didn't live the music the way some did, the message got through; the music was all around you. By the time the Mamas and Papas released "California Dreamin'," we were all doing it. Then Richard Carson, one of the Pikes who'd gone through pledging with me and later moved to the West Coast, came back to Denton for a visit. You couldn't exactly put your finger on it, but he was different. We all noticed it—longer sideburns, a different way of dressing, an ease in his manner. We kidded him a little and made jokes among ourselves, but inside I envied him the freedom he seemed to have found.

I was living pretty expensively, between the parties and the women and the trips to Dallas and keeping up the boat and repairing my car after five or six different accidents—most of which involved a little too much booze. My new roommate during junior year was working for Braniff Airlines at Love Field outside of Dallas and he didn't have to say much to convince me that a job with the airline would beat the onion packing plant at home hands-down. It was a glamorous world, exciting and new. You were eligible for free flights (I'd never ridden on a plane), you wore a good-looking uniform, and you got the chance to meet stewardesses. We all knew about stewardesses.

I was hired as a baggage boy, driving tractors loaded with luggage to and from the planes on the graveyard shift. I kept up with school halfheartedly during the day and squeezed parties in between. One weekend I scored impressive points with my friends by taking a girl on a three-day date to Acapulco. There were other trips down to Mexico as well, and those first few flights were some of the most exciting moments of my life. I'd grip the arms of the seat during takeoff and feel the rush of power go through me. Peering out the window, I'd watch the tiny, cramped world I'd grown up in disappear and I'd know that finally I'd gotten out from under everything that wanted to hold me down — all the small-town pettiness and ignorance and piety that my home and family represented. I was soaring, I was my own man, and I was very pleased with what I'd become.

I began work at Braniff in January 1967, and that spring, while I was taking off for Mexico and making the rounds, of nightclubs in Dallas with a series of stewardesses, Charles Manson was released from McNeil Island Federal Penitentiary in Washington and moved to the Haight-Ashbury section of San Francisco where he spent the spring starting the Family. At that point in my life, if anyone had told me about this short ex-con who'd spent seventeen of his thirty-two years in penal institutions, I'd have written him off as a loser and gone back to the primary business of my life — having a good time.

I worked for Braniff all summer, and as my senior year approached, Denton looked more and more uninviting. I needed a change. Even Dallas night life and discounted flights to Mexico couldn't keep me free from that tight little world I'd grown up in. The final straw came when I totaled my car one night as I was leaving a nightclub and trying to make it through a yellow light. The remains of my Coronet 500, that moving symbol of all I was and hoped to be, brought barely $800 as junk. I decided it was time for a visit to my fraternity buddy Richard Carson in Los Angeles.

I had a date with one of the stewardesses I'd gotten to know at the airport a few days before I left, and when I picked her up that night there was a strange smell in her apartment.

"That's just a pot burning," she winked. I didn't know what she was talking about. Later in the evening, while we were at a dance club, she explained to me that what I'd smelled was marijuana and that we could buy some good stuff from one of the band members. I was intrigued and I was scared. I wanted to please her—and even if weed hadn't been cool at Denton, apparently it was cool here, so I approached the musician nervously and a few minutes later we were on our way back to her place, the proud owners of fifteen dollars' worth of stems and seeds. I'd never seen grass before so I didn't know the difference.

Like most people, I didn't get much out of my first smoke except a scorched throat, but I liked the feel of it, passing the joint back and forth, relaxing, having an excuse to hang loose. When the girl suggested that much better grass was available in California, I agreed to try to bring her back a lid.

A few days later I was leaning to look out the plane window as we started the descent into the Los Angeles Basin. It was smoggy as we crossed over the mountains and the slanting sun turned the haze into a kind of blazing, thick red stew. It was like sinking into the mouth of a volcano. The city seemed to go on forever, and I liked it even before we landed.

From listening to the music you sometimes got the impression that there was nobody in California over thirty. The first thing Richard showed me was The Sunset Strip and I began to think the songs were right. The rows of discotheques and clubs and psychedelic shops were packed with young people, and they looked different from any people I'd ever seen before. The men wore beards and long hair and beads; the girls danced along with nipples outlined beneath their thin blouses. People played flutes on the corner and walked barefoot on the concrete. A girl brushed by me murmuring, "Grass? Acid? Speed?" Rich took me into the famous Whiskey a Go-Go, and as the rock blared I stared at the dancers, couples moving to the beat in the most unabashedly sexual movements I'd ever seen in public. It was a long way from Texas and if freedom was what I'd been looking for, I was certain this was it.

Richard's tour included a visit to a buddy of his named Paul Williams, a young songwriter nobody had heard of at this point. He lived in a tiny little room under a garage on the side of a hill and couldn't even get anyone to listen to his music. He played us one of the songs he was working on. In a few years, he and I would both be famous—for very different reasons.

It seemed like the whole weekend was a rush —we drove all around Los Angeles. We partied and smoked dope, and the California grass did what it was supposed to. The lid I'd promised my stewardess friend was easy to find. The pace was faster than anything I'd ever know back home and the people seemed looser, freer. I felt as if I fit in pretty well, though later Rich would tell me I'd really blown away a girl he knew, when she stopped by his apartment and I stood up and called her "Ma'am" when she came in the room.

Sunday morning Rich's brother Willis, who wanted to be an actor and had changed his name to Ben Brooks in hopes of sounding more professional, took me to church. Knowing my background, I guess he thought it would be what I expected. It was a Religious Science congregation and seemed pretty similar to church at home: lots of talking that meant very little to me. I half-dozed through most of it. On the way home, Willis told me that what he was really into was something called Scientology. The way he explained it, it was a whole new kind of trip that combined the wisdom of some of the Eastern religions with new scientific understanding of brain waves and energy. He threw around a lot of terms like "aware" and "beta" and "karma" and I tried to act interested, but what I was really thinking about was the girls we were planning to see that afternoon. The last thing I wanted to hear was something as complicated and crazy sounding as Willis-Ben's new religion. I couldn't have suspected that later some of these same concepts, reworked by Charles Manson for his own peculiar purposes, would end up directing my whole life.

By the time the weekend was over, I knew what I wanted but it took three more trips before I finally went home to my parents and confronted them with the fact that I was moving to California. They objected all the way up to the moment I got on the plane on August 28. But I knew what I was doing. At last I'd be totally my own man, totally free, without anyone telling me what to do. That was what it boiled down to: I didn't want anyone, ever again, to tell me what to do. It sounded so good. But in twelve months, Charlie Manson would be telling me what to do.

California Dreamin'

I made the move to Los Angeles at a strange time in the history of the youth movement that Charlie and his Family so reflected and finally helped to destroy. The great "summer of love" in San Francisco was just over, already starting to sour, with rip-offs and people OD'ing in the alleys. Charlie and his group had left the Haight months before and started wandering, looking for a home.

The "hippie trip" was already becoming big business, with the mass culture slowly picking up and capitalizing on the counterculture. Aging male movie stars were wearing love beads and letting their hair grow. Computer technicians were starting to sprout beards and mustaches. Beverly Hills lawyers bought grass and served it with the after-dinner drinks. Expensive department stores began selling faded jeans and India-print dresses—at their usual high prices—while middle-class, middle-aged couples went to see professional hippies take off their clothes in *Hair*. Within a few short years, a movement which had seen itself as a radical rejection of the whole materialistic, business-governed American bag had become just another tool of the corporate machine, another way to make a buck.

There were some deeper changes, of course, that went beyond the clothes and the turquoise jewelry and the water beds. The sexual freedom that a few bohemians and radicals and artists had been practicing and advocating for generations became an accepted option within mainstream American mores, at least in the more urban areas. And drugs became a permanent part of the life-style of American young people. Both these changes were all right with me.

My parents had made me promise that if I moved to California I'd finish school, so I enrolled at Cal State Los Angeles in business administration. I'd bought myself a new car on the final trip out before I told them about the decision to move—a yellow 1959 Thunderbird convertible—and now I found an apartment in the Silverlake district just east of Hollywood. It was on an ugly, busy street, but I was on my own and that was all that mattered. The big song at the time was The Doors' "Light My Fire," but I was sure nobody needed to light mine; it was going strong already.

All the Joe College clothes I'd been so proud of in Texas started to look a little square. I wasn't ready to become a hippie—I still thought they were strange and I liked too many of the material things they had no time for—but I let my hair grow a little longer and found myself using the freaked-out jargon that seemed to be the new universal tongue.

During my last year at Denton I'd written a paper on drug addiction. I'd treated it in the usual fifties' manner –

as a bizarre aberration of a few lower-class individuals. It was still in the style of *The Man With the Golden Arm*—as far as I knew. But this was different, all new. Everyone you talked to, everyone your own age anyway, was into grass at least, and often more. People talked a lot about acid: LSD. One of the clubs on the Strip advertised itself as the "acid experience"—but that scared me a little. You heard too many horror stories of people walking out of third-story windows, thinking they could fly, or ending up like drooling vegetables after a bad trip.

Grass was safe, though; grass was good. It gave me a peace I'd never had before—especially in the middle of all the changes that were going on in my life—and was a better high than all the beer I'd guzzled back in Texas. Not that I stopped drinking, but weed was taking the place in my social life that booze had before. Sharing a joint was the basic social ritual between friends, and it was one of the things that set us apart from the square world of cops and parents and teachers.

Shortly after I arrived in Los Angeles, I read an ad in the paper offering a job as salesman for a wig shop in Beverly Hills. "Salesman" turned out to mean walking up and down sidewalks giving girls a card that entitled them to a free wiglet if they came into the shop. There was a gimmick. You had to pay three dollars for styling what was actually about a fifty-cent wiglet, and once the girl was in the shop she got a hard sell for a full wig at considerably more than three dollars. Before long I was one of the in-shop men, doing the hard selling and making so much money that there didn't seem to be much point to staying in school; it just cut into my party time. I quit Cal State.

Life looked good for me in the fall of 1967 — nothing but more money and more women and more fun ahead. Then I got word that my high-school buddy Tommy Caraway had been killed. In Vietnam. I went home to be a pallbearer. I couldn't believe it: Tommy Caraway — whom I'd driven all those back roads with, worked on the sports page with, confided my fledgling sexual exploits with—dead. Death had not been part of the world we'd lived in, not sudden death like this in some jungle half a world away. Only old people died. But there was Tommy in that box. I wish I could say that it made me more politically aware, or finally brought home to me that there were bigger things going on in the world, more important issues than getting high and making money and racing around the Hollywood Hills in my T-Bird, but it didn't. It didn't even particularly affect how I felt about the adult, conservative society around me that had made this war and killed my friend. All it did was make me even more determined to have a good time.

When I got back to L.A. it seemed like the pace kept getting faster and faster. The wig shop moved, and I spent hours building new fixtures and cabinets for Mike and Phil, the owners. They were low on money so I did it all on the promise of payment later when the new shop got established. Rich had moved in with me while I was still at the place in Silverlake. Once I quit school we moved to an apartment in West Hollywood, then to a house on Wonderland Drive, up in Laurel Canyon behind the Strip.

The Canyon was a strange place. Somebody told me it had started as a place for summer cottages back in the first part of the century, when there were still miles of open country between Hollywood and Los Angeles. It still had a little bit of that feeling, with trees and narrow canyons running up into the hills, but now the cottages were run-down shacks jumbled in between expensive houses where actors and writers and musicians lived crammed together on the narrow streets. At the bottom of the hill, just before you reached Sunset Strip, there was a market and restaurant where street people hung out, right alongside movie stars and singers and agents at the tables in the open-air cafe. Sometimes, at a distance, it was hard to tell who were the hippies and who were the show-business types. In the other direction, behind the Canyon, the huge San Fernando Valley spread out, and if you went far enough north and west to the other side, you'd reach the Santa Susana Pass and a run-down movie ranch called Spahn.

I had been sticking to grass since I came to the city — Rich kept telling me I wasn't ready for anything heavier — but when I got back from Texas and putting Tommy in the ground, I decided to try some rosewood seeds our next-door neighbors had brought back from Hawaii.

I wasn't ready for what they did to me. It seemed like everything outside of me came crashing down and everything inside, too—all the frustrations I'd felt at home, all the things that scared me here, all the pressures between what I'd been raised to think and believe and do and what I wanted for myself. Suddenly the whole world seemed to turn blue and threatening. I'd never thought of myself as having violence in me; I always thought I was a happy, gentle kind of person. But as all this pressure started coming down on me, something came rushing up from inside, deep in my gut, something like an explosion—and I wanted to fight back and break and smash and tear into the world and I didn't even know why, except that I felt angry and confused and pushed. I ended up putting my fist through a door. For a long time I was afraid to try any hallucinogens again, afraid of what I'd seen inside myself.

As 1968 began, my life started quietly disintegrating, so quietly I wasn't even aware of it at the time. It began with a car accident one rainy morning on the way to work with Rich, who'd been working at the shop with me for a month or so. Laurel Canyon is tricky, especially when wet, and the friend who was driving us skidded into a head-on collision that messed up my knee badly enough to put me in the hospital for an operation. Although the whole thing didn't seem all that important at the time, the accident and the lawsuit that followed had a number of consequences later—keeping me out of the army, involving me with two lawyers (who would later come to Texas and fight for the right to represent me and obtain the publicity such a trial could bring them), creating an insurance claim that would later be the excuse for a bizarre odyssey back to Death Valley, looking for Charlie after I'd run away from him.

But the most immediate result of the wreck was a visit from my mother. It would be wrong to say I didn't have a good time. We showed her the sights and she was suitably impressed with the house and the furniture and the stereo I was buying. But underneath it all there was tension. I could tell she wasn't happy about the way she sensed I was living, the kind of people who kept coming and going. We'd smoke grass behind her back, and I'd dodge her questions about the girls who spent so much time at the house. After five days she announced she was going home early because she couldn't take the situation anymore. While she was packing, she as much as begged me to come home with her. Strangely enough, a part of me wanted to do what she asked, wanted to go back to the life I'd known, the values that I'd been raised with. But I felt as if doing that would be as much as admitting I'd been wrong, that I'd made a mistake in coming to California in the first place. I wasn't willing to do that.

"I'm never coming home again," I told her. It was the last time I would see her until nineteen months later when I ran away from the desert, out of my mind and responsible for seven deaths.

The car wreck was just the beginning. I started dealing a little grass as well as smoking. Nothing heavy, just enough to supplement what I wasn't being paid at the wig shop. The back wages I was owed piled up so far that I finally took the owners to the Better Business Bureau, and Rich and I decided to start our own shop. We figured if the wiglet gimmick worked for Mike and

CHARLES "TEX" WATSON

Phil, it would work for us. We called our place Love Locs -- love was the big word right then—and opened up in a tiny former beauty parlor on San Vicente off La Cienega. In the meantime, we'd gotten bored with Laurel Canyon and moved out to Malibu, a house right on the beach. The surf practically came up under my bedroom. Now, I told myself, now I would really get it together. Actually, "it" was coming closer and closer to falling apart.

Love Locs was doomed from the start — we didn't know very much about business and had gotten ourselves into a lease that took 20 percent of our profits off the top. After two months we hauled all the wigs and supplies out to Malibu and decided to work from the house. But it was spring and the beach was too inviting. We ended up spending most of our days smoking weed in the sun instead of selling wigs. Finally, to pay the rent, we decided to try dealing grass full time, but we didn't seem to be much better at selling grass than we had been at selling wigs.

I can't look back now and pinpoint at just what moment I "dropped out." For a while we kept telling ourselves that some kind of break was just around the corner, some big score, but all that was really starting to matter was being stoned and going to rock concerts. I'd never been that interested in music, but now the music started to get to me. I'd always thought the hippies were a little strange, but now I started thinking of myself as part of something new, something different. I couldn't have put it into words, but somehow I had made the break from the last ties to my past. I didn't care about working or making money or acquiring things. I just wanted to lie back and ride with the flow. Whatever it meant to be a hippie, I guessed I was one, after all. I was floating free— no more past that mattered, no more future worth worrying about. Just then it was the beach, the bright blue sky, the sun baking through you, and the grass that brought it all together. It was a lazy, late spring and that was all.

I met Manson.

Gentle Children, With Flowers In Their Hair

It began one night when I was driving out Sunset Boulevard toward the beach, heading home to Malibu. By then I'd sold my T-Bird and had an old 1935 Dodge pickup. Hitchhikers were pretty common on Sunset, and I pulled over to pick one up. When he told me his name was Dennis Wilson it didn't mean anything to me, but when he said he was one of the Beach Boys I was impressed. I remembered all those surfing songs banging out of my brother's room back in Copeville and grinned to myself, wondering what he would think if he could see me now — with Dennis Wilson taking a ride in my truck and explaining how he'd wrecked his Ferrari and his Rolls Royce so was having to use his thumb.

When we got to his house in Pacific Palisades he invited me in. Rolling up the long driveway to what had once been Will Rogers's mansion, I played with the idea of what it would be like to tell my brother about the time one of the Beach Boys had me in for coffee. When we went inside it was all I could do to keep my mouth closed. I'd never been in a place like this before—it was a long way from a three-bedroom frame house in Texas.

The first thing I saw when we came into the kitchen was a heavyset, bald-headed man with a big gray beard pouring down his chest, sitting at the table with a few girls. He introduced himself as Dean Moorehouse. Over the next few months Dean and I would become friends, despite the fact he was twice my age. I was to find out that he'd once been a Methodist minister, that up in Ukiah, California, after the Family left San Francisco, he'd gone after Charlie, ready to kill him for seducing his daughter Ruth (the one the Family came to call "Ouisch"). Instead of killing him, though, he ended up worshiping Charlie as Christ, after Charlie turned him on to LSD. Since then, he'd given up whatever Christianity he'd once held and become a kind of wandering guru, teaching a lot of people in the film and music industries that true "awareness" and real "religion" came through opening yourself up with acid. When people became aware, according to Dean, they could be free to die to themselves, to die to their egos. Then they would understand that Charles Manson was the reincarnation of the Son of God. Finding out all this came later, though. That night in the kitchen he was just a fat old man with a greasy beard, trying to look like a hippie.

Almost as soon as I came in he said there was somebody I should meet in the living room. I followed him.

There he was—surrounded by five or six girls—on the floor next to the huge coffee table with a guitar in his hands. He looked up, and the first thing I felt was a sort of gentleness, an embracing kind of acceptance and love.

"This is Charlie," Dean said. "Charlie Manson."

There was a large ashtray full of Lebanese hash sitting in the middle of the coffee table, and pretty soon Charlie and Dean and Dennis and I were lounging back on the oversize sofas, smoking. Nobody said much. As we got stoned, Charlie started playing his music, softly, almost to himself.

Here I was, accepted in a world I'd never even dreamed about, mellow and at my ease. Charlie murmured in the background, something about love, finding love, letting your self love. I suddenly realized that this was what I was looking for: love. Not that my parents and brother and sister hadn't loved me, but somehow, now, that didn't count. I wanted the kind of love they talked about in the songs — the kind of love that didn't ask you to be anything, didn't judge what you were, didn't set up any rules or regulations— the kind of love that just accepted you, let you be yourself, do your thing whatever it was — the kind of love I seemed to be feeling right now, sitting around this coffee table getting zonked on some of the best hash I'd ever had, with a rock star and a fat old hippie and the little guy with the guitar who just kept singing softly, smiling to himself. It occurred to me that all the love in the room was coming from him, from his music.

Suddenly the girls came out of the kitchen and started serving us sandwiches they'd made — organic, full of sprouts and avocado and cheese. It was as if we were kings, just because we were men, and nothing could make them happier than waiting on us, making us happy. We all lay back and listened to Charlie sing to us about love — make love to us and for us with his music. I'd never known such peace.

Late that night at my truck as I was leaving, Dennis smiled and told me to come by anytime, take a swim in the pool, whatever I wanted. I drove out to Malibu, knowing that whatever had been going wrong in my life would be okay now. I'd found what really mattered: love between people, love that made all the old ideas about love as romance — or love as your parents pushing at you — just fade away. Charlie Manson was the first person I'd met who really knew what love was all about.

I came back the next day to swim — and then the day after that. It seemed I was always having some reason to take Sunset into town, and on the way back to Malibu I'd turn up that long driveway. By day, the place was even more impressive—huge ranch house, separate servants' quarters, an Olympic-sized pool and bathhouses set in unbelievably lush tropical gardens and surrounded by gigantic eucalyptus. Gradually the peculiar domestic situation at the house sorted out: Dennis leased it, but he spent a lot of time away on tour. While he was gone, Dean Moorehouse unofficially ran the place. It turned out that Charlie didn't actually live there; he spent most of his time out at Spahn Movie Ranch, just coming into town every so often to see the girls, go to parties, and promote his singing career. Three or four Family women lived at the house, along with several other girls who were friends of Dennis's.

Life was very laid back in that Sunset scene. The girls went out on garbage runs every day, getting perfectly good food that was tossed out into the bins behind Brentwood and Palisades supermarkets. Eventually I started taking them on their runs in my truck and I found out that before it was wrecked they'd used Dennis's Rolls Royce for their foraging trips to the dumpsters.

We smoked dope a lot, we lay around, and we listened to music. The music was always there, always going, singing and making a world—saying there was something beyond the senses, something brighter, wilder, truer—saying that love was all that really mattered.

People came and went, a peculiar mix of young dropouts like me, drug dealers, and people in the entertainment business. It was a strange time in Hollywood. It had become chic to play the hippie game, and the children of the big stars partied with gurus like Dean and Charlie and listened to them and bought drugs from them and took hippie kids to bed and let them drive their expensive cars and crash in their Bel Air mansions. Everybody felt aware and free. After August 1969, all that would change and those gentle children with flowers in their hair and tabs of acid in their pockets would suddenly seem menacing and dangerous. The Beverly Hills-Hollywood circuit would snap shut like a trap.

Eventually Rich and I realized we weren't going to be able to keep paying rent on the Malibu house. We hadn't sold anything, grass or wigs, in months. When we had an opportunity to sublet the place, we did—and after a couple of weeks of staying with a dope dealer I'd gotten to know in Westwood Village, I piled all my clothes and stereo and tools and wigs into the back of my truck and moved into Dennis's house. Everything looked good: I didn't have to pay any rent, I had my own room in a mansion, and the girls took care of the men as if they were princes. It was hard to believe that six months ago I'd been on the verge of going back to Texas with my tail between my legs.

Now life was one big party. Rock musicians and hopeful singers like Charlie, actors and hopeful actors, girls who didn't do anything, producers like Terry Melcher (Doris Day's son), talent people, managers like Gregg Jakobson, and stars' children would all come over to the house and it would be a drug circus. Charlie always managed to show up for the parties. And he did it well, playing the free, spontaneous child, the holy fool, turning his self-effacing charm on a pretty young celebrity's daughter with twenty different kinds of pills in her purse, giving her a ring and asking her to come join his Love Family. She kept the ring but drove home in her sports car with her boyfriend.

I'd been afraid of anything heavier than grass since my experience with the rosewood seeds, but seeing all these beautiful, sophisticated people who could spend half their lives on one kind of high or another made me think again.

The first thing I tried was cannabanol, a synthetic hash. This time there was no blue fog, no sense of things collapsing on me, no violence welling up from inside; this time it was all love, a tremendous physical feeling of oneness and caring. It was what I'd felt that first night listening to Charlie sing, only more. It was love that flowed through your body like thick syrup in your veins, warming wherever it went, making you so "one" with the person you were with that you'd have laid down your own life for him or her, and it wouldn't have mattered because you were so "one" that the distinctions between the two of you hardly existed anymore. It was a kind of connection even deeper and better than sex.

I saw how crazy I'd been to turn my back on all this good feeling, all this awareness and openness and love, just because of one bad trip. I tried peyote, then mescaline, then speed, then some synthetics you smoked with grass. Suddenly the whole world opened up like a flower that I'd never seen except as a bud. Colors came alive, throbbing with energy; simple objects became fascinating in their textures and shapes and mass; things like the sky or a blade of grass or a girl's hair could make you laugh for crazy joy. Time and space suddenly weren't the constants they'd always been. When you were on speed, time could race past you, jerk to dizzy starts and stops, leap over itself all together sometimes. Solid objects could become fluid, dripping into new forms like something out of a Surrealist painting. Music wasn't just sound; it became a physical thing, bathing you, rolling over you like breakers, sweeping you up and carrying you with it while you felt it inside as well, picking up the beat of your heart until the music was truly "within you and without you," just like the Beatles sang.

Dean Moorehouse took me on my first acid trip. Now it wasn't just the external world I saw differently. It seemed the LSD opened me up to what was inside me as well. Suddenly I saw myself as I really was, all the elements, all my past and hang-ups and fears and attitudes laid out in the searing light of truth. Again, there was no fear, no violence, just letting myself go with the changes, letting things slip away like glass beads falling slowly through my fingers. You could be at peace because nothing had to be hassled anymore, nothing had to be fought. It might hurt to let go of some of that past conditioning, some of what you'd been, but it would heal in the wash of what you could be free to become.

When I started taking acid, Charlie was not an important figure in my life, not personally. But Dean talked about him constantly, was practically an evangelist for the "gospel according to Charlie," and the Family girls carried on the theme. They said that each one of us has an ego, a desire to assert ourselves and our existence as something separate and cut off from the rest of life around us. We hang on to that ego, thinking that independent self is the only thing that lets us survive, thinking without it we'd perish. But the truth is that we all are one, all part of the same organic whole, no separate me or you, just ripples in the one wave that is life. True freedom means giving up ourselves, letting that old ego die so we can be free of the self that keeps us from one another, keeps us from life itself. "Cease to exist," Charlie sang in one of the songs he'd written. "Cease to exist, come say you love me." The girls repeated it, over and over—cease to exist, kill your ego, die— so that once you cease to be, you can be free to totally love, totally come together.

They kept urging me to join the Family, the life they had together with Charlie. Charlie, they said, had died more completely than anyone, not only in this life but long before, on a cross. In becoming one with him, in dying to ourselves so we could really unite with him, we could become one with love itself, with "God." Every trip Dean and I took together, it all made more and more sense. But I still clung to my ego, my sense of self— sometimes in fear, sometimes in stubbornness. I wanted the love they were talking about, but I wasn't sure I could pay the price.

When Charlie came around, it almost seemed possible. When he looked at you and saw everything there was inside of you and loved you anyway, it seemed worth the risk. One day, when he'd driven down to the house in a school bus he and the Family had decorated with hanging silks and beads and a huge wall-to-wall bed, I walked up to him and gave him the keys to my truck and said that it and everything else I had were his. For years I'd struggled to accumulate all I could: the right cars, the right clothes, the right things that would somehow complete what I thought was missing inside me. Now I gave all that, everything I had, to Charlie. Suddenly I felt very free. There was nothing tying me down, nothing I had to be responsible for. Charlie's girls had been right; material things imprisoned us, poisoned us, kept us going in the false sense of self that took away our freedom to die.

By this time, more of Dennis's friends had moved into his house, including Gregg Jakobson, who'd recently left his wife. One night on the way to a party two of them gave me my first sniff of cocaine. At first all it did was make my gums and nose numb, like going to the dentist, but then the rush came and once more life was better, "with a little help from my friends."

Life flowed on through a long easy summer. Then, in August, while Dennis was away on tour again, Dean started putting pressure on some of the women in the house to go to bed with him. Word got back to Dennis, and pretty soon his manager told us that the lease was due to expire and we'd all have to be out. When Dennis returned to L.A. he avoided us, moving into a place at Malibu with Gregg, not far from the beach house Rich and I had leased.

I had nowhere to go, so when Dean told me he had to drive up to Ukiah for trial on an LSD charge I decided to go along. Until the problem with the women, Dean had continued to be a sort of spiritual advisor to Dennis, and he apparently still had that status with Terry Melcher, because he told me that Terry was loaning us his Jaguar XKE and a credit card for the trip north.

We picked up the car one morning at Terry's house in Benedict Canyon, a rambling ranch-style place at 10050 Cielo Drive. It was the first time I'd been to the house, but it would not be the last.

Everywhere we stopped on our way up the coast there were "flower children." San Francisco may have soured, and the flowers may have been turning to plastic in Los Angeles, but that didn't stop the kids. We'd talk to them about Charlie and love and tell them to stop by Spahn Ranch anytime they came south. I'd never driven anything like Melcher 's XKE and, roaring past Atascadero on the freeway several hundred miles north of L.A., I was pulled over and ticketed. As we drove on I crumpled up the citation and tossed it out the window. I never planned to be anywhere near Atascadero again. Two years later I'd be back, though — as an inmate of the state mental hospital there, nearly dead.

Dean's trial lasted only two days and then he was released on appeal. We were staying with a family he knew in Ukiah, of them freaks: parents and kids—and while we sat around turning on together I thought that this was what a real family should be like. The parents were laid back, sharing their dope with their children — everybody easy and no hang-ups. More and more, I identified my own family with only the negative things I'd felt were holding me down; more and more I forgot the love and caring that had been there, maybe never talked about much, but always there.

It seemed a shame to waste the car on such a short trip, so we stayed on for a few weeks, driving all over the Bay area, visiting friends of Dean's. I remember one night especially, making love to the Indian wife of a guru friend of his in the car and then driving back home with her to Dean and her husband and children to spend the night.

While we were in Ukiah, Charlie and some of the girls brought up the bus and it broke down on the way to San Francisco. It was around this time that several murders took place in the area. As intriguing as the connection might seem, however, no one in the Family was involved; we didn't even hear about them, as far as I can remember. All we knew at that point were love and Charlie and dope. The only death we cared about was dying to ourselves, inside.

Apparently I hadn't died enough, because when Charlie sent some of the girls to me to suggest I give him Terry Melcher's credit card so the bus could be repaired, something from my Texas past about honesty nagged at me enough that I wouldn't let him use it. Charlie wasn't happy—this proved I wasn't dead yet; I still had the delusion it was possible for anyone to own anything.

When we finally got back to Los Angeles, dropping acid all the way, Dean and I went to see Dennis at his place on the beach. He was still furious that Moorehouse had tried to seduce the women at the Sunset house and somehow, even though I hadn't been involved, being Dean's friend was enough to turn Dennis off to me as well. It was beginning to look like Charlie had been right—just because a person dressed like a hippie or did dope, it didn't mean he wasn't still part of the uptight American dream world of things and money and rules, still locked into ego, still undead.

Dean and I started looking for a place to stay.

While I was gone, Rich Carson had moved back into our place in Malibu with some friends of his, but they had no money for the next month's rent and were going to have to move out themselves. Charlie didn't want us at Spahn Ranch. I still had too much ego, he said, and he didn't want a horny old man like Dean going after his young loves.

Suddenly I felt very alone, and somehow Charlie seemed like the only hope I had. I had to prove myself to him. Finally I had him come down from Spahn with the bus, and he and I and the girls completely cleaned out the Malibu house, not just the rest of my possessions that were stored there but all the furniture I'd rented with the house. Driving back to the Valley we passed out things to anyone we met—I made a present of a two-hundred-dollar camera to a young hitchhiker we picked up—finally leaving most of the busload with an Eastern religious commune in the hills above the movie ranch.

Charlie still didn't want Dean and me with his people. Finally he gave us a tent and told us we could stay down by a creek below the ranch itself. But we were on our own, he said; we were no part of his Family. It was a long way from a mansion on Sunset Boulevard, but it was all that seemed left for me—I had no place else to go. The Family let us eat with them occasionally, and once or twice Charlie and the girls came down to our tent in the evenings and sang.

Then Dean had to go back to Ukiah for another trial and I was left by myself in the little tent by the muddy creek. At night, alone in the stillness, I could hear the sounds of laughter and singing and love drifting down from the Western sets on the hill.

Family

Although I'd heard about Spahn Ranch soon after I first met Charlie, I had never actually been there until the day Dean and I picked up Terry Melcher's XKE at the Cielo Drive house and then stopped by the ranch for several days before continuing north to Ukiah. The fact that I first saw both places—10050 Cielo Drive and Spahn — within an hour of each other on the same day, driving directly to the ranch from Benedict Canyon, is one of those strange twists of fate that could have no meaning for me until much later.

Spahn Movie Ranch had once been used extensively as a location for Western films and some early television series. Any kid who grew up watching half-hour shoot-'em-ups in the early fifties will recognize those strange dry hills, covered with huge sandy boulders. By the time Charlie and his Family moved in, the place had gone to seed and was only used for an occasional Marlboro commercial. The real business was renting out horses, mainly to teenagers, usually on weekends.

Shortly after Dean Moorehouse went to Ukiah the second time (and never returned), Charlie took me up to the ranch house to meet George Spahn, the blind owner of the place. The old man was sitting in a chair with one of his little dogs in his lap, his cane beside him. Charlie introduced me and explained that I was a good mechanic and might be able to get some of the old trucks that George had sitting around the ranch running again. I didn't realize it at the time, but most of the people that Charlie brought out to Spahn, at least the ones he told George about, were supposedly there to help work the place. I'm not sure Spahn even knew about a lot of the others, especially the women, but if he did, Charlie kept him satisfied by giving him Lynette "Squeaky" Fromme — one of the original San Francisco Family members who was eighteen at the time — as his housekeeper. She also spied on the eighty-year-old man for Charlie, as well as making love to him.

When I spoke to Spahn he recognized my accent and dubbed me "Tex," a nickname that was quickly picked up by the Family. Part of Manson's method of deprogramming us, of breaking our ties to the past and our usual perceptions of ourselves and the world, was giving all Family members new names. I think, in my case, there was an added reason: there could only be one Charlie.

He decided that hard work was the best way to get rid of my negative karma. True to his word to George, he had me start by fixing up some of the old trucks. It was an uphill fight; most of them were past repairing, and I'd just think I had one going and something else would go wrong with it. A bigger project was what came to be known as the In Case Place, a small house —some might say "shack"—that he had me build for him at the back of the ranch. As the name suggests, the little cabin was where Charlie and the others were supposed to escape in case the ranch was ever raided. I spent two months working on it — digging out a floor and putting it together with scrap materials the girls would throw down the bank to me. Never in all those two months did it occur to me to wonder why —with all this talk of peace and love — Charlie thought he'd need a place to hide from the police. When I wasn't repairing trucks or building the house, he kept me busy going down to the Valley on garbage runs with some of the girls and even helping George Spahn's son repair fences on the property.

After several weeks of work, Charlie let me move up the hill to the movie sets and ranch buildings where the Family lived. After he directed one of the girls, Mary Brunner, to be my special "love," I began to feel a little less like an outsider, but there was still pressure to prove myself, especially with some of the women constantly preaching to me that I wasn't as dead as I should be, that I hadn't reached awareness.

Mary was a blond Scandinavian type, a year older than I was, prettier than most of the pictures published of her later would show. Like all the Manson women—taught that their only purpose in life was taking care of men and having babies—she knew how to make you feel good.

During the months that Mary and I were more or less together, I learned practically nothing about her past. The past was nonexistent for the Family, something to discard along with all the materialistic, middle-class programming and the ego that it had built. The Family lived in the present, the moment and its fancies, not questioning where we'd come from, who we'd been. People simply were who they were, and it never occurred to anyone to wonder how or why. If one day one suddenly changed his or her name (as many of the girls did more than once) and took on a new personality, then you just rode with it.

Our only real history was an assortment of occasional fragments we picked up of Charlie's own past: his time in jail, the fact that he reached "beta" (a Scientologist term for the highest state of mental and spiritual awareness), his discovery of love in a San Francisco park when a young boy handed him a flower.

As for Mary, I did gradually learn that she was the very first Family member. Charlie had met her walking her dog outside the gates of the University of California at Berkeley where she'd been a librarian. She had been present when he discovered his "true identity" on an LSD trip and she had been the "Magdalene" weeping at his feet as he "hung on the cross." It was to her apartment that Charlie started bringing more "young loves"—at first over her objections, I sensed—and when the Family began wandering in the bus, she'd quit her job and joined them. She had been the first of the Family women to bear a child by Charlie — Michael Manson. Charlie himself had delivered the baby, with the rest of the Family watching.

I began to realize how alone I'd felt for the past year on my own in Los Angeles. Rich had been a good friend to me, and there'd been girls and friends from the wig shop and people you got to know through drug deals and parties. But now I saw how empty and plastic all that had been—people spending time with people but never knowing them, people using people but never caring, people like Dennis Wilson making you think they were your friends and then turning their backs on you. The Family was different. Here were people you could count on, people you could share everything with, people you could become so one with that you'd give your life for them and know they'd do the same for you.

It may have something to do with the attitudes I was raised with, or maybe it's just part of the person I am, but I've never been very introspective. I've tended to see life pretty much as what it appears to be on the surface, see it in terms of events and places and things, not trying to analyze inner feelings and motives, my own or anyone else's. Charlie presented himself to me as incarnate love, and I accepted it without question. The girls talked about being free and one—and I believed it. I did begin to notice unique personalities, though, within the inner core of the Family, individual egos and characteristics that survived even as we worked to destroy all traces of ourselves and become perfect blanks, reflecting our father, Charlie.

It was most obvious in the girl we called "Sadie Mae Glutz"—Susan Denise Atkins. Susan had one of those strange faces that was sometimes pretty and sometimes very homely, and there was something about her that reminded me of a lonely child desperately anxious to be liked and noticed and important. Sometimes it seemed as if she even wanted to fight Charlie himself for the center of the stage. Then he'd have to discipline her with a quick slap or jerk at her hair. Later, when the Beatles' song "Sexy Sadie" came out, the words fit her so well that it made us all sure the group had to be singing directly to us: "Sexy Sadie . . . you came along to turn everyone on . . . you broke the rules, you laid it down for all to see . . . ." Susan - Sadie had broken all the rules, sexually, and liked to talk about her experience and lack of inhibitions. Sometimes it seemed to me that she saw her sexuality as just one more way to draw attention to herself. Susan was the evangelist of the group, always praising Charlie, repeating his teaching, urging the rest of us to give ourselves to him totally, even while her own ego was fighting back sometimes, asserting itself against his domination. It wasn't so much that she resisted doing what Charlie told her; she just wanted to be special; she refused to be annihilated.

Then there was Leslie Van Houten, in some ways the prettiest of the women. Leslie was like a little girl — emotional, easily hurt, spontaneous, willing to do whatever she felt like doing, without thinking. The other girls ordered her around a lot and she accepted it, falling into her "mountain folk" role, complete with lazy, exaggerated accent and pretended helplessness. Underneath all the crazy playacting and little-girl manner, I felt she was always genuinely afraid of

Charlie. There was no question that she would do anything he told her to, just as she obeyed Susan. I was the only one she'd talk back to.

Patricia Krenwinkel was different. We called her "Katie," and even though she was the sweetest of the girls, none of the men except Charlie ever got involved with her sexually. She was a little standoffish and, probably more important, unattractive. When Charlie started trying to get bikers involved with the Family by offering them girls, they all complained that Katie was too hairy. For all the talk about love and oneness, I think she must have felt the rejection from the men and that made her all the more devoted to Charlie—no matter what the others thought, Charlie loved her, and would make love to her. Why shouldn't she do anything he asked?

Katie — Leslie — Sadie—and another girl, a quiet, motherly little hippie named Linda who wouldn't even join the Family until five weeks before the murders — and me: Tex Watson. Why us? Why were we willing to be sent out into the night with guns and knives? More important, why did we say yes—all of us but Linda—when Charlie told us to kill? There was the acid and the domination and the Helter Skelter doctrine that gave a reason for it all, but still—why? Maybe for Katie it was gratitude and devotion to Charlie, who accepted her when no other man would. With Susan-Sadie perhaps it was a matter of keeping in the middle of the action, close to Charlie and his plans. Maybe Leslie did what she was told on the second night because she was a born follower and afraid. And perhaps I had to prove to these women that I was just as dead as they were, just as open to Charlie, just as one, just as aware.

Whatever the reasons, that was all a year away. Now it was love — love that meant death — and *freedom* — *freedom* that meant total slavery to Charles Manson. We weren't the only ones, of course; even though later estimates of the Family's size were exaggerated, there were eventually about thirty of us.

I'd gotten to know some of the girls while I was living at Dennis Wilson's house with them: Ouisch (Dean Moorehouse's daughter Ruth) — one of the young girls Charlie kept for himself; Brenda McCann (her real name was Nancy Pitman) — of all the women probably the most like Charlie, the most blanked out. The time would come when she and I would be so completely dead, no thoughts in her head, no thoughts in mine, that we could look into each other's faces when we were on acid and see our own reflection staring back at us. There was also Gypsy (Catherine Share) —a raven-haired free spirit who sang and played the violin. Others I met for the first time at the ranch: Squeaky (Lynette Fromme) —so devoted to Charlie that she would shut herself away with an eighty-year old man most of the time, being his eyes and Charlie's ear; Dianne Lake — the sad little girl whom Charlie kept hitting and whiping but who loved him anyway; Sandra Good — she was pregnant but still seemed to think she could somehow keep herself for Manson, maybe hoped she could someday have him for herself alone.

There were men, too, though never as many. "Clem" (Steve Grogan) was Charlie's favorite of them. He was severely retarded and acted as if he were about five years old, parroting everything Charlie said and following the girls around with a stupid sort of grin on his face. Charlie told us he should be an example for everyone because he needed very little deprogramming. He was innocent, like a little child before his mother got to him and killed his soul and laid the whole sick society's trip on him. "No sense is sense," Charlie often said; and Clem hardly ever made sense.

Paul Watkins — later freed from Manson's control by Paul Crockett, the old Scientologist in Death Valley — was Charlie's chief recruiter when I arrived at Spahn Ranch. He was good-looking and smooth and useful, since Charlie was always anxious to get himself new young loves and build up the Family. A young girl might come up horseback riding and end up with Paul in one of the ranch buildings. He would make love to her and draw her into the beautiful world we all shared. Then Charlie would give her acid and pretty soon she'd be living with the rest of us, learning how to die. Brooks Poston, who was later sent to the desert with Paul and came under Crockett's influence as well, began as a stable hand at the ranch, shoveling manure. He was always weak and unreliable as far as Charlie was concerned, because on his first acid trip he laid on a mattress for three days in his own excrement, completely out of his mind.

Of the others, I probably became closest to T. J. (Tom Walleman), a sort of gypsy in his late twenties whom Charlie had picked as his right-hand until the trip changed from love to death and T. J. split when people started being killed. On the fringes of the Family were ranch hands like Juan Flynn, the Panamanian cowboy who stuck around even after Charlie threatened him—partly because he liked the sex and partly out of stubbornness.

This was the Family that was going to protect me from the loneliness the city had come to mean to me; these were the people who would populate my world, the people I would live with, make love with, drop acid with, finally kill with. It was a strange collection—Charlie would later refer to us as the ones society didn't want and threw away—but who we were really didn't matter all that much. The only personality that counted for anything was Charlie: Charlie-our father, Charlie-our god, Charlie-our selves.

Magical Mystery Tour

So much has been written about Charles Manson, so many interpretations made of what he was, what he represented in our world, how he became what he is. During his trial he told the court that he was whatever the outside world made him; he was a monster created out of the deepest fears of the establishment. Perhaps so. That fall of 1968 I know he became what all of us lost souls and discards in the Family were searching for: somebody to love. More important, he was somebody to love us, to teach us, to tell us what to do with our confused lives.

What can I say about him that hasn't already been told a dozen times? He was short-five-foot-two— with a strangely high voice. He was, as some of the girls put it, always changing. One moment his movements would be slow, almost trancelike, and then the next he could be exploding with a violent energy that shook off him to set everything around him on fire. He changed his hair and beard constantly, and with each change he could be born anew—Hollywood slicker, jail tough, rock star, guru, child, tramp, angel, devil, son of God. He was a magician; he charmed-in the original sense of the word-— and he had an uncanny ability to meet a person and immediately psyche him out, understand his deepest fears and hang-ups, his vulnerabilities. It was as though he could see through you with the all-encompassing eye of God.

Like a cat with one ear cocked even in sleep, Charlie was always aware, tensed even in stillness, always picking up the smallest details in any situation. He told us it came from being in prison so long—you never knew where a knife might be coming from. His awareness seemed not only intensive—able to look inside you and know all that you were —but comprehensive: holding all the elements of a situation in his consciousness at once.

His eyes were hypnotic; they could wash you in love and gentleness or they could terrorize you, like the face of hell itself. He knew the tricks he could play with his face and he used the force of his undivided attention consciously, recognizing how difficult it is for most people to be the focus of that kind of energy and powerful quiet.

As for the magical powers with animals which some of the Family later claimed for him, I only know that I once saw him walk through a gully full of rattlesnakes, gliding among them and touching them gently on the tails. None of them struck. I think this had less to do with magic than with the fact that animals of all kinds can pick up on the fear in a person. Charlie had no fear left in him and somehow that was calming to other creatures.

All through that strange hot summer at Spahn Ranch, camped among the crumbling sets of a former dream, we were children at play, living the fantasies we made. It was, as the Beatles sang, a "Magical Mystery Tour," and Charlie was our guide. We shared a huge pile of clothes among us and, like Charlie, we'd change roles constantly. One day we'd dress up as cowboys, the next we might be Leslie's mountain folk, the day after that we were cool Hollywood types in soft shirts and sunglasses. With all the playacting and running around, it's surprising that any work ever got done, but it did. One of Charlie's primary rules was keeping up a good front around guests and customers at Spahn. A lot of the girls were kept in semi-seclusion on the back part of the property. If anyone in the Family was visible, he was supposed to be working, making the place look like a real ranch, not a commune. We'd groom the horses along with Juan and the other stable hands, clean up around the buildings, do odd jobs, and sometimes the girls would serve as guides on weekends. If the customers seemed likely candidates for the Family, they'd find their guides spending a lot of the tour talking about this fantastic, loving guy named Charlie. If the visitors were interested and if they were girls, they'd sometimes end up sleeping with Charlie or Paul. If the newcomer was male, one or two of the girls might take him back into one of the shacks or ravines and give him a taste of what Charlie's kind of love was all about.

I still had a fair number of inhibitions about sex when I came to the Family. My hang-ups hadn't kept me from wanting and getting all the women I could. That was excitement enough, and my tastes were ordinary—I didn't think about more than one woman at a time or those wilder variations that were snickered about in college bull sessions. It was only after I moved up to the ranch house from the creek that I discovered that the Family's sexual habits went way beyond what I was used to. I knew Mary gave herself to me completely once Manson gave the okay, and pretty soon it became obvious that the other girls were equally willing, at least most of them, but I still wasn't ready for my first experiences of Family group lovemaking. "That's just your father," the girls would taunt me. "That's just your mother talking." My mother probably wouldn't have had words in her vocabulary to describe what was going on.

There was a room in the back of the ranch house totally lined with mattresses, and those members of the Family who were free, who felt "at one" together, usually slept there in whatever combinations worked out on a particular night. Since there were a lot more girls than men, the alternatives were obvious. I eventually got used to making love to one or more of the women, while a few feet away Paul or T. J. or Clem would be involved with some of the others. In time, it worked out so that—perhaps once a month—the whole inner circle would make love together, but even then there were never more than eight or twelve of us, since a lot of the girls never became free enough to participate. Contrary to some of the information published later, even in these larger groups there were limits to what went on. Despite some of what has been written about Manson's methods of breaking down inhibitions, I never saw any male homosexual activity in the Family; in fact, I heard Charlie preach against it several times. I never saw or heard anything about the sexual initiations that were reported, either—Charlie supposedly performing perverse sex acts with a new member while the rest of us watched. Sex was an important tool in Charlie's deprogramming, and he did tell us that as long as we had any inhibitions we still weren't dead, we were still playing back what our parents had programmed into us. But he also taught us that women were made for men to love and to have babies, so some forms of sexual expression just didn't fit his teaching. I think some of the more bizarre stories about sex at Spahn that eventually became accepted as fact were just exaggerated attempts by Sadie and others to shock or impress outsiders.

Charlie did occasionally stage an orgy for the benefit of selected men he hoped to lure into the Family. Such events were rare and more often than not they backfired. Instead of being drawn in by the sexual circus, the visitors were often driven away— all too aware that it was Charlie who decided the cast and the action. Most men, no matter how carefully Charlie thought he had prepared them, weren't ready to submit that completely.

The lack of sexual discrimination among hard-core Family members was not so much gross animalism as it was simply a physical parallel to the lack of emotional favoritism and attachment that Charlie taught and insisted on. As long as we loved any one person more than the others, we weren't truly dead and the Family wasn't one. We were all certain we believed what Charlie said and we repeated it and tried to practice it, but the irony remained that every one of the girls, at least on an emotional level, quite clearly preferred Charlie to the other men and they were all anxious to be his sexual partners.

Charlie's peculiar sexual power over women was something I didn't think about at the time and I still don't understand completely. True, many of the women he gathered around him were not the kind that would get a lot of attention from most men, but not all of Charlie's girls were unattractive. Some—like Ruth Ann Moorehouse or Leslie Van Houten— were conventionally beautiful. From the girls' jokes about the sexual prowess of outsiders like Danny DeCarlo, a member of the Straight Satan motorcycle club which Manson later tried to involve in the Family's preparations for Helter Skelter, it seemed as if Charlie did not provide the ultimate in the physical side of sex. The attraction must have been psychological and emotional, perhaps even spiritual. Whatever it was, it worked, at least when it was combined with acid trips and the pressure of the group.

I think the acid was the key, not just to the women but to all of us; it combined with Charlie's diabolically forceful personality and his joint-nurtured insight to turn rebellious American kids into pliant slaves.

All your life you had been taught a certain way to think, a certain set of moral values, a certain perspective on the world—how it worked, what was real. Most of these things you never questioned; it never occurred to you that they were a framework in your head which you used to understand and organize the constant sensory perceptions and information and experience that were being poured into your brain. You didn't think about this framework because it wasn't what you thought about, it was the way you thought. You assumed that all this programming, this way of looking at the raw data your mind was given to process, was simply true, in fact, was truth.

But acid changed all this by letting you see your familiar little mental world as separate from the sensory data it arranged in such neat, conventional packages. Acid shattered the connection between raw experience and your handy preprogrammed responses and judgments and categories. It wasn't just a matter of radically altered perceptions, though that was part of it. Space and time melted in your vision to take new forms; common objects could become monsters or revelations of God. It wasn't just increased sensory awareness, either, though when you were on acid you could see microscopic and riveting detail in the most ordinary things and you could sometimes hear a whispered conversation in a building halfway across the ranch. These changes were only the beginning, however; the real core of the acid experience was the dissolution of the thought process itself -- suddenly you could deal with the increasingly intensive and vivid perceptions your environment was feeding you in any number of new ways. There were no judgments to be made (". . . there is no right, there is no wrong, there is no crime, there is no sin . . ." went one of Charlie's songs). Things that had always seemed real were revealed as empty shells, while fantasies were suddenly substantial, powerful.

What we didn't realize in all this, but what Charlie obviously knew (probably more through his own observation than any real study), was the fact that LSD also makes a person extremely open to suggestion and the force of a stronger personality. We thought we were discovering a new world, a new truth beyond our senses and the lie that was given us by our parents and our society. We never saw that this new world was Charlie's world and this new truth was Charlie's truth, made in his image. He had become the creator and through the acid we became his creation, his true believers, finally his slaves.

Love was always the key word: love as nothingness, love as death. Each night the Family would eat together, smoke a little grass or hash, often drop acid. Then after the meal we'd all sit in a circle to listen to Charlie sing his songs and preach to us. He called it deprogramming, that is, stripping away all the untruth and ego and confusion that our parents and our society had laid on us from the moment we were born, stripping it away to get back to a purity and nothingness that was ours when we first came into the world.

His teaching at first seemed complex, its terminology a strange mixture of Eastern religion, Scientology and pop psychology, but at its core was a simple, powerful message. Everything was one, he said. The programming which our personal histories had built into us put barriers between us and the realization of that oneness, kept us broken in separate fragments torn from our connection with the Whole. We kept seeing "you" and "me," when in reality there was only "it," the one. The only way to break down those barriers between ourselves (or the fantasy of self) and true oneness, true unity, was love.

Charlie defined love as totally giving ourselves to each other and to him without reservation, without clinging to anything of ourselves. The only way to find that kind of love was to completely kill the ego in us, recognize that we were truly nothing independent of the Whole, and realize that the idea that we had some sort of separate identity was illusion. To become one, we first had to become individually nothing, undergo a psychological and spiritual death that burned out any independent personality within us and left only a blank, dead head.

Once you were dead in the head, you could truly love because there was nothing left of you, nothing but the oneness which was love itself to fill the void. When you were one it no longer mattered if this or that part of the Whole died, if you died or if someone else died, because the Whole remained. As bizarre as Charlie's teaching might sound to an outsider, it was compelling to us. The more acid we took and the more we listened, the more obvious and inevitable it all seemed. It was not just a matter of belief, either. We lived it, we experienced what Charlie talked about. The time came when we could look into each other's faces and see our own features, when we could be sitting together and suddenly all think the same thought. It was as if we shared one common brain, when we could project something — a visit, people bringing up some grass — and it would happen; the friend would appear, someone would knock on the door with a lid. You couldn't argue with evidence like that.

There was no talk of killing, not yet. But Charlie's theology of death — death in life, death as life — laid a compelling groundwork for murder. After the killings, people were shocked and horrified that we expressed no feeling for the victims, no remorse. Why should we, if the death and life of any particular individual had no more meaning than breaking off a minute piece of some cosmic cookie? Why should we, if killing the body simply opened the soul to a new experience of the one — the Whole?

Like any good philosopher, Charlie had other and more practical teaching as well. A lot of it revolved around the place of the female. For someone who attracted so many of them, Manson had an amazingly low view of women. Women were the primary source of ego programming; thus no mother in the Family was allowed to take care of her own child and the women were always supposed to talk to the babies in nonsense syllables to avoid contaminating them. Women built the prisons; women caused the wars; women upset the natural order by refusing to keep to their intended place — slaves to men. Charlie seemed to have a special hatred for women as mothers, even though he taught that childbearing was one of their major purposes in life. This probably had something to do with his feelings about his own mother, though he never talked about her, never told us she had been an alcoholic and a prostitute. The closest he came to breaking his silence was in some of his song lyrics: ". . . I am a mechanical boy, I am my mother's boy ...."

Men, on the other hand, were supposed to be kings. Our kingship was something he liked to talk about. He told us we were at that moment in the process of becoming kings; he was making us kings. As for the girls, what they needed most was a king to serve, a king to love them. "That's all there is," he'd say. "If you don't have somebody to love you, you don't have nothing."

It was a special kind of kingship he offered us, however. As he said again and again, we only became kings by becoming slaves to all. "All" usually translated as "Charlie." His domination would begin in small things—not even direct requests. Usually a subtle indication of what he wanted was enough. Then it would build until we were slaves to his every comment, every whim, every suggestion. Why should we refuse him anything? Whatever we did for him was an act of love, love for "God" himself. It was a privilege to serve.

And it was a curious deity we were serving. While it meant nothing for a human being to die, Charlie would fly into a rage if we killed an insect. While there was supposedly no right or wrong, only what was, Charlie was a fanatical vegetarian because, he said, killing an animal or eating a dead animal was a crime. While love was supposed to be the meaning of everything, the source of our oneness together, Charlie spent a lot of his time talking about fear.

Watershed: The White Album

Fear.

To Charlie, it was the source of awareness, of connection, of clarity. Wild animals live in a constant state of fear, he told us, and they don't miss anything in their environment; they achieve total awareness of what is around them and in the process are totally lacking in self-consciousness. That was how we should be.

Yet we should overcome our fear as well, push ourselves to its limits until nothing frightened us anymore. Later, in the summer and fall of 1969, we'd begin to live out this part of Manson's teaching—crawling through people's darkened houses as they slept, racing suicidally over mountain roads in dune buggies, spattering ourselves with blood and gore in orgies of death. But for now it was mostly talk.

It could also be a game. Charlie liked to walk up to people at Spahn and hand them a gun. "Go ahead," he'd tell them, "shoot me." When he was refused, Charlie would take back the gun and grin strangely: "Well, now I have the right to kill you."

Charlie never allowed calendars or clocks at Spahn—time meant nothing when you lived an eternal now—so it's hard to place events during that long summer and fall of our love trip. Days and weeks overlapped, the acid and the repetition folding time in on itself and losing particulars in the creases. Charlie still hoped to become a recording star; he kept writing songs and sometimes he would disappear for an evening, gone into Hollywood for a party with Gregg or some of the other industry people he'd met through Dennis Wilson. One night Gregg and Terry Melcher came out to the ranch and we all sat around a fire back behind the buildings and ate and smoked dope together and Charlie sang his songs with the girls. We knew what he meant when he sang:

A home is where you're happy,

Not where you don't belong.

Burn all your bridges,

Leave your old self behind;

You can do what you want to do

If you're strong in your mind.

This was our home, this was where we belonged — with Charlie. We were happy and, to our ears, Charlie's music was perfect, flawless, the girls' random harmonies blending into a oneness that was beauty itself. Terry didn't seem too impressed, though.

The broken-down bus had never managed to get back to the ranch, so sometime during that disjointed summer Charlie decided to send T. J. and me up to San

Jose to try to get it repaired. Hitchhiking up the coast, we found out it wasn't just the heads and freaks and movie colony who had discovered acid—one truck driver who picked us up had enough LSD in his cab to turn on half the state. As we drove along, getting down into the drug, I suddenly took a cigarette and let it burn into the palm of my hand. I was fascinated by the way the skin scorched and blistered as the red-hot ash poked deeper and deeper. I felt absolutely no pain. As the stench of burning skin filled the cab I held up my branded stigma and showed it to the driver. "Hey," I grinned, "what d'ya think of that?" "Whatever turns you on," he answered. Middle America had gone through a few changes of its own.

After two trips north and countless hassles, we finally brought the bus back down to Spahn, picking up hitchhikers all along the way. We were Pied Pipers full of stories about love and acid and changes and the beautiful thing happening at the ranch. When we got back there was big news: Charlie had actually managed to talk Gregg Jakobson into arranging a one-day recording session for him at a little studio in the Valley. At last Charlie would get his chance, the destiny that was rightfully his. Now the music that all the young people heard would be his music and he would open up their minds just like he had ours; love would triumph and the old world of ego and separation would just fade away. Charlie was going to be a star; we were all certain it would only be a matter of months before his face was on the cover of Rolling Stone. Actually, it took him almost two years to make that cover and when he did it wasn't for his singing. The headline read: "Charles Manson . . . the Most Dangerous Man Alive."

The whole Family went down together for the taping and we brought all our instruments with us—guitars, drums, tams. We gathered around the mikes at Charlie's feet, singing with him just like we did in the evenings after dinner. "Cease to exist," we all sang. "Cease to exist, come say you love me." We knew we were part of something bigger than any album ever cut, bigger than Dennis Wilson and his overage Beach Boys had ever been, bigger even than the Beatles themselves, because this was more than just music. This was Charlie's message to the world; this was Charlie giving his soul to all the free children that were waiting for him whether they knew it or not. If the crew in the dinky little studio gave each other any cynical looks over this ragged band of hippies swaying back and forth and making up harmony as they went, we didn't notice.

During one of the breaks, Charlie started strumming his guitar and scat singing. At first it was just nonsense syllables: "Digh-de-day, digh-dow-doi, digh-tu-dai, de-tew-digh." Then slowly one phrase replaced all the others: "Digh-tew-day, dightew-day . . . ." Suddenly we realized he was singing, "Die today . . ." over and over, smiling to himself.

Weeks passed, then months, and we heard nothing more about Charlie's recording career-no more tapings, no contracts, no albums. A bitterness began to set in. If Charlie wasn't getting the recognition he deserved, it had to be because someone was cheating him out of it, because some one of those rich, fat-cat, music-industry hippies had betrayed his trust. By the next spring — after the Family trip had changed from love to Apocalypse, from ego death to real death and Helter Skelter — we'd have hard evidence of that betrayal. The Beach Boys released a new song, "Never Learn Not to Love," that was very similar to Charlie's "Cease to Exist." The lyric of the chorus was "Cease to resist," and Charlie never got a cent of royalties on his song. The Family noted bitterly that the Beach Boys had managed to turn the central theme of Charlie's message into a corny sex lyric. Once more Dennis Wilson had failed us—as had Gregg Jakobson, who with all his industry contacts and talk and enthusiasm hadn't been able to get any of his big-time friends interested in Charlie's music.

For some reason, the frustration slowly came to center on Terry Melcher, Doris Day's son, the record producer who'd been getting spiritual counsel from Dean Moorehouse until Dean was locked up in Ukiah on his acid bust. "How does it feel to be one of the beautiful people?" the Beatles had asked in one of their songs and Terry should have known—he had all the money and material things he could want and lived in the rambling ranch house on the hill in Benedict Canyon at 10050 Cielo Drive. Terry, Charlie told us, had made him some big promises and then never come through. Terry, Charlie said, didn't care about anything but money. After his first visit to the ranch to hear Charlie's music, Melcher had come up again with another producer who owned a mobile recording unit, apparently trying to push Charlie off on him. Charlie had given the guy some LSD and the trip had scared him so badly that we never saw him again. That was the last thing Terry ever did for us. Gradually, it seemed clearer and clearer, at least to us, that Terry Melcher was the one who had failed Charlie, who had led him along and then betrayed him, who had kept his music from the world.

There were other frustrations for Charlie as well. The girls, at least some of them, would never let themselves die, would never completely let go of their egos and their demands for his special love. More and more he'd lash out at them or withdraw into black silences. Some of the ranch hands were taking stories to old George Spahn, trying to turn him against Charlie and get him to throw us off the ranch. And Charlie's friends in Los Angeles started avoiding him; the Beverly Hills parties stopped.

By that fall it was obvious that Manson was ready for some kind of change, and when a young girl named Catherine Gillies joined the Family and started talking about an isolated ranch her grandmother owned in Death Valley, Charlie decided we should all go up and check it out. We filled up the bus with as much of our stuff as it would hold and started for the desert. The only food we had on the way was ten cases of canned chop suey that had gone bad. Every time someone opened one of the cans it would stink up the whole bus, but some people were hungry enough to eat the stuff anyway.

Catherine directed us down the road to within about five miles of Golar Wash, as far as the bus could go. We piled everything on our backs and started walking. When we reached the Wash—standing there in the blazing desert sun with all our gear dumped around us—the seven miles of rocks and gullies and dried-up waterfalls did not look very inviting, but Charlie said to move out, so we did.

We found the two ranches as I've already described them, and Charlie decided we would camp at the lower one, Myers, the one that belonged to Catherine's grandmother, since Barker Ranch above it looked as though someone used it fairly regularly. Myers Ranch lacked a lot of the comforts of Spahn, but Charlie seemed happier, more at peace, so that made us all feel better, too. Up in the desert, cut off from everything except the blazing sun and the dry hills and the acid and each other, it was even easier to let the past die, let everything you had been fade away like water vapor on the sand. It was a self-contained world as Spahn Ranch had never been, and up here it didn't seem to matter quite so much that our so-called friends in Hollywood had let us down. In the desert we could truly be one.

But Charles wasn't satisfied for long. Even though he'd gone to Arlene Barker, who owned the upper ranch, and done his number about being with the Beach Boys and given her the gold record and gotten permission for us to camp there, one day he announced we were leaving — all of us except Brooks Poston and a girl named Juanita. Juanita had come to the Family early in the summer, giving Charlie her Dodge van and most of a $10,000 inheritance. It was her money that had enabled us to finally pay to have the bus repaired and bring it back from San Jose. In fact, we'd done more than just repair it; we'd bought a lot of garish imported tapestries and hangings and incense pots — combined with silk sheets we'd ripped off from Dennis Wilson's house, mattresses that filled the whole back half of the thing (including my king-sized one from the Malibu house), and scrap furniture we'd collected to make a kind of living room in the front. All that made our bus a regular gypsy wagon, smells and colors and patterns everywhere.

And now it was back to the bus, Charlie announced; we were going to Sacramento to see "Candy Man," an ex-con friend of his. So we piled everything on our backs again and trekked the twelve miles down to the bus and headed out for the state capital.

I've never known exactly what Charlie was looking for during the aimless weeks we hung around Sacramento. People would drift in and out but no one new joined the Family. We'd visit some of Charlie's old friends for a while, then take off for a few days in the bus. It was as if Charlie were waiting for some kind of direction, something to happen. He still gave himself to us with his love and was the center of our life together as always — he was our life itself — but now he seemed to draw into himself sometimes. There seemed to be something going on in his head that he couldn't share with us. When a fellow whom Sadie had picked up fresh out of jail proceeded to infect her with some kind of skin disease (and through her, all the rest of us), Charlie was furious and decided it was time we went back to Spahn. Whatever it was he was after, he'd have to find it there, at the ranch where we'd had our best times together, close to the city and the music industry that had rejected him. Whatever he was waiting for would be there.

We got back to Spahn Ranch sometime in the third week of November. There was a letter waiting for me that had somehow gotten forwarded through several addresses to the ranch: I was ordered to report for an army physical in Los Angeles on December 2, my birthday. That crisp official notice seemed like a strange intrusion into my world. Squeaky had stayed behind with George and she had news, for us too: Gregg Jakobson was in jail on some kind of drug charge.

Charlie decided I should go to Terry Melcher and see if he would be willing to help bail Gregg out, even if he wouldn't do anything for us. I don't think Charlie was as much concerned about Gregg as he was still hanging on to the hope that somehow Jakobson would be able to do something for him professionally. At the time it didn't occur to me to ask him why he was sending me to Melcher. I just did what I was told. The next morning I hitchhiked into Beverly Hills and went to 10050 Cielo Drive for the second time. I pushed the gate button as I'd seen Dean do and wandered up to the back door. The driveway was fairly long and I took it slowly, listening to see if anybody was up yet. Ten months later, on that same driveway, I would kill a human being for the first time in my life—the first, but not the last.

The maid remembered me from my earlier visit with Dean and brought me into the kitchen. I was still pretty grubby from bumming around in the bus and while I sat there alone, waiting for her to get Terry, I felt out of place, over my head, especially when a glamorous star, who was living there with Terry at the time, walked in on me and demanded to know what I was doing there. Even after I mentioned Gregg it was obvious she didn't think I belonged in that kitchen.

Terry was friendlier, but I got the feeling he wasn't particularly interested in getting involved. He said it was Saturday and there was no way he could get his hands on any money. As his driver took me down to the bottom of the hill I thought how our Family would give their very lives for each other, but these people wouldn't even spoil their Saturday to help each other out. No wonder they'd treated Charlie so badly.

Hitchhiking back out to the ranch, my thoughts drifted from the plastic, pretty people like Terry (and the stars with whom he surrounded himself) to Charlie and all of us in his Family — all of us so tight, one without distinction. We shared everything — clothing, food, work, bodies — even shared one common soul. My mind drifted on until suddenly I was jolted by the realization that for the first time in what seemed like years, I was alone, by myself, not with Charlie or anyone else in the Family. There was just me, Charles Watson, standing on the curb with my thumb out in the bright November sunlight. There was something exhilarating about it. I couldn't explain why, but I suddenly felt incredibly free, with a sense of endless possibility. I could cross the street and hitch back into L.A.; I could get on a freeway and head back home if I felt like it; I could just sit down and bake in the sun. I'd forgotten what it was like to feel the freedom that being on your own, responsible to no one, can give you. But that was what I'd come to Los Angeles for in the first place, that kind of freedom. Why did I suddenly feel like I was just discovering it all over again?

I watched the cars going by, the people in them, a lot of them my own age. What did they have that I didn't? It was something I was losing, but what? What was it that made them look free and alive in a way I wasn't? Suddenly it hit me — they had lives of their own, they could choose, they had at least the illusion of self. I looked back over the past months, life in the Family at Spahn, in the desert, wandering around in the bus — all this talk about dying to yourself, killing your ego — I knew now there was nothing left of me, and for the first time that was a frightening thought. The terrible sense of confusion and disintegration that came with it was even worse.

Everything I'd been taking as gospel for eight months suddenly seemed bizarre and improbable. I didn't want to die; it couldn't be true life, this annihilation. Yet it had to be true, all of it. I'd experienced it as true. But, then, how could I say I'd experienced anything? I no longer existed, not in the sense that the people passing me on the street existed, had lives, made choices. Everything had seemed so certain, but now there was panic. What was happening to me?

When I got back to the ranch, I didn't say anything to anyone, but somewhere inside of me was a pounding, inescapable certainty: I was losing my mind. All the realities I'd known on the acid and all the things we'd shared in the Family were just madness. But they couldn't be madness. Charlie had given them to us and Charlie knew what was true; he loved me and he wouldn't lie to me. But could he be wrong? I didn't know what to believe.

I don't know if Charlie could sense what was going on inside me — it seemed he must be able to see it, the break, the disloyalty, the self pushing to life again — but later that afternoon he asked me to go to Topanga Canyon with him, a little place just off the Pacific Coast Highway where a guy we'd met while we were wandering around up north had a house. The two of us hardly spoke on the way there. I was spinning crazily inside, afraid to say anything, and Charlie seemed distracted, into himself, as he had been so much over the past month.

As I sank back on the pillows of a huge bed that hung on chains from the ceiling of the strange Topanga cabin-tall windows sweeping up to a pointed roof, oak trees smothering the place outside — I barely heard the conversation. I ate a couple of hash brownies as they were passed and tried to calm the racing in my head by leaning back and listening to the music, taking in the light sifting through the trees and tall windows and rocking gently in the suspended bed. I hadn't thought of my friend Richard Carson in a long time, but now his face kept forming in my mind. Maybe if I talked to him, maybe if I talked to someone who was outside of all this, who was free of it, I could clear up the conflict that was tearing my brain apart.

I knew there was a phone in the kitchen, and all I had to do was get up and go to it and call Rich. Charlie Manson didn't own me, Charlie Manson couldn't stop me — but a physical weight seemed to hold me down, press me into the cushions. Then the fellow we were visiting told Charlie he had a copy of the newest Beatles' album, just released, and asked if he had heard it. Charlie hadn't. He had always been obsessed with the Beatles, partly in admiration, partly, I think, in jealousy for the ultimate success and power that they represented in the rock world. The jacket was tossed around and I noticed it was solid white, the only title on it was simply THE BEATLES, in raised lettering that was almost invisible unless you angled it against the light. Charlie always got down into music, listening with a peculiar intensity, and he may have reached for the sheet of lyrics that came with the album at some point, but as the songs rolled over us — "Piggies," "Sexy Sadie," "Blackbird," "Revolution," "Helter Skelter" — I only half heard them and I was too busy with my own turmoil to notice much of Charlie's reaction to the music in what became known as the White Album.

Finally I went into the kitchen and called Rich. The first thing I blurted out was "Man, I think I'm going nuts." I tried to explain some of what had been going on, the changes in me, the way my self seemed to have evaporated in the flame of Charlie's strong personality. When Rich said he had to take his army physical the same time I did, I heard myself telling him to come and pick me up at a little store on the corner of Topanga and the highway in an hour. When I put down the receiver I couldn't believe what I'd done. But I had; I had decided to leave Charlie. I didn't even go back into the other room, I just opened the back door and headed for the highway. As I left, I heard one of the new Beatles' songs blasting out after me:

> *Look out helter skelter helter skelter Helter skelter*
>
> *Look out helter skelter She's coming down fast*
>
> *Yes she is*
>
> *Yes she is.*

I had no idea that, as I ran away from him, Charlie had found what he'd been looking for these many months, maybe for his whole life.

"Helter Skelter . . . She's coming down fast . . . Yes she is!"

Happy in Hollywood

I realized how much I'd changed by the expression on Rich's face when he picked me up at the Topanga Feed Store. Clean-cut Charles Watson was now Manson's child Tex — with a scraggly beard and long hair and grubby clothes. All the way into town I kept talking, even though I knew what I was rattling off probably didn't make any sense at all to Rich. I had to talk about it, had to try to catch up with the confusion that chased me from one end of my brain to the other.

Rich and his brother Willis, the aspiring actor, had a place in Highland Park, a Chicano district northeast of L.A., and when we got there I found they'd managed to save a few of my things from the Malibu house before Charlie and I cleaned it out and gave everything away. It was strange to see things that were mine again; I'd forgotten what ownership was like and somehow it was reassuring. If there were these physical objects that belonged to me, then "*me*" must exist, must be different from all the other "*yous*" around me. They fixed up a bed for me in the corner of the living room, and suddenly I'd come full circle: I was back staying with the Carson brothers just as I had been a little over a year before when I'd first come to Los Angeles, determined to be free and alive and different.

The only practical thing I accomplished during the week we waited for our army physicals was to go to the doctor who'd operated on my knee after the accident and get a letter saying I had a disability and should be granted a medical deferment. The letter (and a little faking on my part) worked. I was granted 1-Y classification—but Rich passed the physical and went ahead and enlisted the same day rather than wait around in limbo until he was drafted.

With Rich gone and Willis at work most of the time, I got pretty bored. I'd arranged to buy a kilo of grass from the dealer who'd been supplying the Family—he fronted the dope with a vending-machine company and people said he was with the Mafia—but I'd sold what wasn't used, so there wasn't even grass to keep me company.

Finally I called a stewardess I knew in Dallas and arranged to spend a Saturday with her the next time she had a layover in Los Angeles. When I appeared at her hotel in the old 1952 Chevy that Rich had left me, with my wild mane of hair and old jeans and boots, she and the girl friend she had with her were stunned. She must have assumed I'd made it big in California—she didn't even work very hard to hide her disappointment. I drove the two of them around town, trying to make up for her embarrassment by taking them to Dennis's house, Beverly Hills, Bel Air, the Strip, and by talking about all the show-business people I knew. These two Texas girls were not impressed. Finally I decided I'd take them to meet Terry. We drove up Benedict Canyon and for the third time I went into that gate at 10050 Cielo Drive.

There was no one home and as we drove back to the airport I realized that they probably thought I just made up a story about knowing people in Hollywood or being friends with the celebrities who lived at the top of Cielo Drive. Even the lunch I'd bought them in Beverly Hills hadn't done the trick.

For the first time, I was embarrassed by how I looked and found myself wanting to go back, back to what I'd had and been before I met Manson, back to all the things I'd worked so hard to get rid of in the Family. I wanted to look sharp and have nice things and money and be with beautiful women like these, women with a little style, instead of all the hippie girls that followed Charlie.

I decided to call up an old girl friend of Rich's who lived in Hollywood. Her name was Luella and I'd gotten to know her casually while Rich and I were still living at the house on the beach. During the week we were waiting for our army physicals, he'd taken me to see her once and, even though they were still sleeping together until he left for boot camp, I felt she'd been especially friendly to me that day. Right now I needed a friend.

I got a lover. The first time I hitchhiked over to her apartment I ended up moving in. Luella was like a lot of good-looking, hip (but not hippie) women living in Hollywood at that time. She didn't have a real job; she kept herself going by dealing a little grass and LSD among her friends — nothing big time but enough to get by. She had an old Hollywood-Spanish apartment with eucalyptus trees all around and a patio that overlooked the driveway to an exclusive private club for professional magicians and entertainment stars. Sometimes we'd sunbathe on the deck, drinking beer and smoking grass while we watched all the big limousines drive up for parties, dumping out beautiful people whom we could never quite recognize.

It was an easy life that Luella and I fell into. Combining her contacts with mine, we found we could sell a lot more dope than she'd been doing on her own. We charged $15 a lid on grass that we bought from our vending-machine friend in $95 kilos (2.2 lbs.) and then broke up into 36 lids. We discovered affluence: a new stereo system and records (one of the first albums we bought was the Beatles' White Album, and we played it over and over until I knew it by heart), expensive clothes, clubs and restaurants where you laid down five bucks just for a beer. I even had my hair cut and started getting it styled by a friend I'd known back in my wig-shop days. And there were parties. As our dealing got more extensive, I ended up keeping different batches of grass in numbered olive jars, since each kilo had its own distinct taste and high, and when people came over to party we'd give them a choice, eventually all the way from number one to number eight. I made a gigantic "bong"—a water pipe-out of some bamboo that grew on the property. As we'd sit around that huge pipe, sucking the water-smoothed smoke of some choice Colombian gold, I'd lean back and tell myself that this was really the life. Whatever had made me think I wanted to spend my time out in the hills someplace—with Charlie telling me what to do?

Yet it was unnerving; every time I turned around I'd be reminded of him. The people we met, the people we sold to and partied with, all of them seemed to fit what Charlie had told us about how people—especially Hollywood types — really were. It was as if everyone I came in contact with and everywhere I went, Charlie had already been there before, already met them and laid it all out for me: the shallowness, the plastic, the willingness to rip you off, the concern with masks and self and money. Sometimes I felt as though he were always with me, thinking my thoughts for me — or his through me. Every situation seemed to bring up some fragment of Charlie's gospel and sometimes I'd feel ashamed for letting my ego come to life again so easily, for getting caught in money and things so quickly.

Playing it happy in Hollywood was not without its problems. Luella had fallen in love with me. After what I'd experienced in the Family, I wasn't ready to limit myself to one woman and although I thought I probably loved her, I couldn't mean it in the exclusive way that she did. I kept seeing and sleeping with other girls, eventually including another one of Rich's old lovers who took me up with her to visit him in Fort Ord and then took me to bed. While Luella lay on the Hollywood deck by herself, watching the limos roll up the drive to the neighboring club, the three of us parked out next to Rich's barracks at the fort, smoking dope and passing joints through the windows to his buddies inside. While

Luella sat home and listened to records and got stoned, I'd be out on the town with other women. I finally convinced her to start dating other guys as well, but she was never happy about it, not even when I tried using some of Charlie's lines on her.

Except for improving her drug business, it seemed that I was pretty much bad news for Luella. After we'd been together for a while she had to go to Mexico for an abortion that was messed up so badly she ended up spending a week at the U.C.L.A. Medical Center. Then, when I decided to show her a special good time, just for the two of us, and took her on a trip down through Mexico and back up to Palm Springs, we got caught in a dust storm in the desert and I smashed her VW into the back of a truck. The car was totaled and she got a bad gash on her head. But she didn't throw me out. We kept dropping acid and making love and having late breakfasts in the seedy restaurants on Hollywood Boulevard and spending those short winter afternoons on the sun deck watching the limousines.

I think she could tell I was getting more and more restless. No matter how many times I told myself that this was what I wanted, that this was where I belonged, I knew Charlie still had a hold on me. The conflict wouldn't let up: Luella and dealing and Hollywood and money that would get you whatever you wanted—or Charlie and the Family and self-denial, rejecting money, wearing old clothes, and eating whatever you could scrounge up a good deal of the time. As ironic as it sounds now, the moral choice seemed to be Charlie (even though he said there was no right or no wrong). My self indulgent world in the city never gave me peace.

It was as though Charlie kept pulling me back, slowly but persistently, even though we'd had no contact since I walked out the back door of that Topanga Canyon cabin. I tried to fight it, but it was no use; he wouldn't let go of me. He'd seen the world I was living in and he'd warned me, and I found it just what he'd said it would be. Even though a part of me liked it, enjoyed all the things I'd been denying myself, it wouldn't work—I couldn't make it work. Nine months with the Family had made too deep a mark on me.

Finally one day I picked up the phone and called the ranch. Even before I dialed, I think I'd decided to go back to Charlie.

Revolution/Revelation

If anyone had asked me in March of 1969 why I was going back to Manson, I would have said I had no choice. Every day I stayed away from him I felt like I was running, running away from the place I was supposed to be, running away from changes that were necessary for me. Charlie was my destiny.

Even when I talked to them on the phone, the Family women sounded different. All they could talk about was Helter Skelter. I knew the title from the Beatles' White Album, but I wasn't sure what they all meant when they kept insisting that "Helter Skelter is coming down fast, and we're getting ready for it." Everything had changed, they told me as they babbled on about a club they were starting and about buying dune buggies and about the White Album which explained everything, laid everything out—and that I'd understand if I'd just come out and talk to Charlie.

The next day I appeared at Spahn Ranch with my styled hair and my silk shirt and leather jacket and I felt like there were two of me standing there—the old Tex whom Charlie and the girls were so glad to see and Charles from Hollywood, noticing the dust that was getting on his expensive leather shoes.

That night I saw the club. It was one of the old ranch buildings painted all black inside, with a huge parachute covering the ceiling and black lights and posters and HELTER SKELTER and other lines from Beatles' songs scrawled all over the walls in luminous paint. There was a large jar in one corner marked DONATIONS. "That's so we can buy things to get ready for Helter Skelter when it comes down," one of the girls explained. Most of the people were Family, but there were a few outsiders too, everybody drinking beer and smoking grass and some of us dropping acid. The White Album was blasting from the sound system until Charlie got up and started performing some new songs of his, things he'd written since I'd left the Family three months before. I didn't completely understand what was going on, but the new songs seemed to borrow a lot of phrases and ideas from the White Album; they were all about Helter Skelter and being time for someone to rise and somebody else to flee to the desert. There was one tune the whole Family joined in on, repeating the chorus over and over: "You better get your dune buggy ready . . . you better get your dune buggy ready."

Then everybody started dancing, Susan-Sadie in the middle of things doing her go-go number, while Charlie and the others sang at the top of their lungs and the psychedelic posters throbbed with their sickly colors in the black light. I was home.

Home had changed some. During the week that followed I commuted between Luella and the ranch—trying to talk her into coming with me, fighting her insistence that I forget Charlie and stay with her in Hollywood, freaking out some of our friends by taking them out to meet the Family (Luella refused to go past the front gate) —and during that strange, fractured week I discovered that even more had been turned around than I first thought. Through the long summer of 1968 it had been all love; now the Family was talking about getting weapons and preparing for some kind of black-white Armageddon. Earlier Charlie had preached oneness in the Family, how we didn't need anyone in the outside world (in fact, we'd gone to the desert to escape that world). Now he was making a concerted effort to get members of some of California's motorcycle gangs to join us, especially one group called the Straight Satans. Then Charlie had been against materialism, money, and things, but now the Family was scraping together all the money it could get its hands on, using every device—from the club itself (which turned out to be a fund raiser for buying dune buggies) to another idea Charlie had for putting his young loves to work as topless go-go dancers.

Ever since I'd known him, Charlie had occasionally mentioned that eventually there would be a bloody conflict between whites and blacks. But a lot of people were saying that—hadn't Watts been the beginning? He'd also made it clear that he thought blacks were inferior to whites and only created to serve them, but this kind of thing had never been a major part of his teaching. Now "Helter Skelter is coming down fast" was the main theme of everything he said, every song he wrote, and it didn't take long to figure out that the black-white terrorism and Helter Skelter meant pretty much the same thing: violent revolution. And now, Charlie was saying, it would be "blackie's turn to win," the karma would roll, and the blacks would end up on top as the establishment.

I didn't understand a lot of it, especially when he started talking about the messages the Beatles were sending him through their music, but I knew where I belonged. When Luella finally refused to have anything to do with the Family, I hitchhiked out to the ranch with just the clothes on my back and asked Charlie to let me join him again.

He had plenty of work for me. The dune buggies the Family was acquiring needed work and customizing to Charlie's special purpose: escape to the desert when Helter Skelter came down. And the girls, Mary particularly, drew me back into the Family's love. I spent my time working on the buggies, dropping acid, sleeping with the group, and making love when the drugs didn't space me so far out that I couldn't function. Every night we'd listen to Charlie sing his new songs and teach us about Helter Skelter. Gradually it began to come together for me.

The two sources of this new truth of Charlie's seemed to be the Bible and the Beatles' White Album, the one he'd heard for the first time that day in Topanga when I ran away from him. Although I got it in bits and pieces, some from the women and some from Manson himself, it turned out to be a remarkably complicated yet consistent thing that he had discovered and developed in the three months we'd been apart.

The central doctrine of Charlie's new teaching was Helter Skelter —Armageddon, the Last War on the Face of the Earth, the ultimate battle between blacks and whites in which the entire white race would be annihilated. As the Beatles sang, this was not some event in the distant future, it was "coming down fast." We were living in the last few months, weeks, perhaps days, of the old order.

Although, as he had always taught, Charlie still insisted that blacks were less evolved than whites and therefore only fit to be their slaves, he said that now all the centuries of oppression and exploitation for blackie were over, his karma had turned, and it was time for him to rise and to win.

The rebellion would begin with a few isolated incidents in which blacks would slip out of the Watts ghetto (for some reason Helter Skelter always began in Los Angeles) and into the establishment, pig neighborhoods like Beverly Hills or Bel Air, where they would perform murders so hideous—stabbing, mutilation, messages written on the walls in the victims' blood—that the white establishment would be thrown into mass paranoia and go on a rampage in the ghetto. They would slaughter thousands of blacks, but actually only manage to eliminate all the Uncle Toms, since the "true black race" (sometimes Charlie thought they were the Black

Muslims, sometimes the Panthers) would have hidden, waiting for their moment.

After the orgy of killing ended, true blackie would come out of hiding and say to whitey: "Look here; see what you've done to my people." This would divide the white community between hippies and liberals on one side and conservatives on the other, and they would launch a fratricidal war that would make the War Between the States look tame by comparison, a war that would divide families, with parents shooting their own children and children slitting the throats of their parents. When it was done, the few whites that were left would be killed off by the blacks and that would be the end of the white race—except for a chosen few who would have escaped all this by going into secret hiding in the desert and under the desert—led by Jesus Christ.

Who were these chosen ones? The Family. And we already knew that Charlie was Jesus Christ.

Charlie said that during all the battle and slaughter, the Family, the chosen ones, would go down under the desert into the Bottomless Pit (spoken of in both Scripture and in Hopi legend) where there is a city of gold and the lake of life with its twelve trees. While there, we would multiply to 144,000 people. This was no mean feat for a Family of less than forty, but necessary according to the way Charlie read chapter 9 of the Revelation of Saint John, and when blackie finally got complete control he'd blow it. He'd realize he couldn't run the world, realize he wasn't good for anything but serving whitey and copying what he did. So the blacks would turn to the only white man left with the smarts to help them; they would turn to Charlie, to Jesus Christ, who would lead the 144,000 chosen people out of the Pit to rule the world forever.

It was exciting, amazing stuff Charlie was teaching, and we'd sit around him for hours as he told us about the land of milk and honey we'd find underneath the desert and enjoy while the world above us was soaked in blood. It was coming soon, he kept insisting, very soon; the Beatles knew it and had made it clear to anyone with the ears to hear: "Look out . . . Helter skelter . . . She's coming down fast . . . Yes she is."

That wasn't all the Beatles knew, either, Charlie added. They knew that Jesus Christ had returned to earth and was somewhere near Los Angeles. Their White Album, he taught, was both a message to this returned Jesus to speak out, to call the chosen, and a preparation for Helter Skelter—planting the seed and setting the stage for the message that Charlie himself was supposed to give the world in an album he would produce, an album that would light the fuse the Beatles had prepared. It was all there in the music, he'd say; just listen to the music. Didn't they have a song about "Sexy Sadie" that described Susan Atkins to a tee, long after Charlie had christened her Sadie Mae Glutz? Didn't they tell blackie it was time for him to rise up, when in their song "Blackbird" they said: "Blackbird singing in the dead of night . . . . /All your life/You were only waiting for this moment to arise . . . "?

And there was more, much more. The proof that the Beatles knew about Charlie, knew that he was in Los Angeles and were urging him to speak out, to sing the truth to the world, was in their song "Honey Pie":

Oh honey pie my position is tragic

Come and show me the magic

Of your Hollywood song . . . .

Obviously they wanted Charlie to make his album. And if they weren't so exhausted from their fruitless trip to find the true Jesus (Charlie) in the Maharishi Mahesh Yogi in India (whom they had written off as "the fool on the hill" in an earlier song that was referred to in the White Album's song "Glass Onion"), they would come looking for him in California—they'd join him. After all, didn't they say as much when in "Honey Pie" they sang: "I'm in love but I'm lazy"? They even went so far as to beg Charlie to come to them in England:

> *Oh honey pie you are driving me frantic*
>
> *Sail across the Atlantic*
>
> *To be where you belong . . . .*

And if that weren't enough to show their encouragement to Charlie to speak the word and make his album, in "I Will" they cried out to him:

> *And when at last I find you*
>
> *Your song will fill the air*

> *Sing it loud so I can hear you*
>
> *Make it easy to be near you . . . .*

There were other songs in the White Album in which the meanings were even less obscure. "Piggies"—complete with oinks in the background — described the pigs — establishment whites in their formal clothes — out for the evening with their piggie spouses — and said that "what they need's a damn good whacking," a phrase that Charlie especially liked. "Revolution 1" had lyrics that were printed in the album as:

> *You say you want a revolution*
>
> *But when you talk about destruction*
>
> *Don't you know that you can count me out.*

But when you listened to the record a voice clearly sang "in" immediately afterward, saying—according to Charlie—that while they had been on a peace-and-love trip before, now (even if they couldn't admit it to the pig establishment) the Beatles were ready for the violence of Armageddon, waiting for Charlie to sing the word that would set it off, as they added later in the song:

> *You say you got a real solution*
>
> *Well you know*
>
> *We'd all love to see the plan .*

Then there was the song "Helter Skelter" itself. None of us had any way of knowing that in England this was another term for a slide in an amusement park. When Charlie interpreted lines like "When I get to the bottom I go back to the top of the slide . . ." as a description of our coming back up out of the Bottomless Pit, it seemed to make sense to us, as it did when he used other parts of the song to plot out our escape route to the desert.

To Charlie, however, the most significant band on the album wasn't a song at all. "Revolution 9" was a strange collage of taped sounds and snatches of music-warfare, church hymns, crying babies, football games, BBC announcers, recited dance names, rock music and on and on-thrown together in overlapping patterns that made it either pointless noise or secret code, depending on your point of view.

Charlie pointed out the repetition of the word rise, first whispered strangely, then screamed until almost unrecognizable. This was the Beatles' way of calling blackie to rise up and begin Helter Skelter, he said, and it was no coincidence that RISE was printed in blood on the walls the night of the second murders, along with HELTER SKELTER, just as PIG had been scrawled on the door of the house on Cielo Drive in Sharon Tate's blood.

He showed us how the same weird chord that ended the song "Piggies" appeared later in "Revolution 9," followed by the sound of machine-gun fire and the screams of the dying. The interpretation was obvious. Most important, because it tied together the two parts of Charlie's apocalyptic puzzle, was the constant repetition of the chant "number nine, number nine" throughout the piece. This, Charlie said, referred to the ninth chapter of the last book of the Bible-Revelation 9—in which lay both the prophecy of what was now coming down and its explanation.

I don't know how Charlie happened to discover the ninth chapter of the Apocalypse of John, but its florid imagery and graphic symbols of death and destruction fit both his purposes and his style only too well. Christian scholars are divided over the exact meaning of this strange picture of death and destruction let loose on the world in the form of avenging angels sent to punish the evils of mankind. But to Charlie this one chapter contained all the basic elements of his Helter Skelter doctrine, spelled out clearly and validated by divine imprimatur. The fact that the rest of the Bible had absolutely no meaning in our life in the Family did not lessen its authority in the least when Charlie chose to use it to his advantage.

Where the Scripture spoke of four angels, Charlie saw the Beatles, prophets bringing the word of Helter Skelter and preparing the way for Christ (Manson) to lead the chosen people away to safety. The avenging locusts that are mentioned were also a reference to the rock group, he said, since locusts and "beatles" were virtually the same. In the King James Version that Charlie used, these locusts are described in verses 7 and 8 as having faces like men but the hair of women, and it seemed to be a clear description of the Beatles' long hair, while the "breastplates of iron" were their electric guitars. The fire and brimstone recorded as pouring from the mouths of the horses in verse 17 were to Charlie the symbolic power of the Beatles' music to ignite Helter Skelter.

As for the "seal of God" on the foreheads of some men that keeps them safe from the plagues of the angels (verse 4), Charlie never explained what it was, but he made it clear that he would be able to see it, and it would divide those who were for him from those who were against him and who would thus die. He also found references to the dune buggies we were gathering and to the motorcycle gangs he was trying to recruit into the Family in the passage's descriptions of "horses prepared unto battle" and horsemen that would roam the earth, spreading destruction. As for the one-third of mankind that the writings say will be destroyed, Charlie interpreted them as the white race, wiped out in Helter Skelter for "worship of idols of gold, silver, bronze, stone and wood" (verse 20)-cars, houses, and money, according to Charlie.

Finally, and most importantly, there was a fifth angel given the key to the shaft leading down into the Abyss, the Bottomless Pit. Charlie himself was that fifth angel, he taught us, and he would lead us, his chosen, into the safety of that Pit. Although he never told us (perhaps he didn't know), the translation of this angel's name—Abaddon in the Hebrew, Apollyon in the Greek—is "destroyer."

One other element I didn't learn until a few months later was the fact that Terry Melcher also figured in all this.

During the months I was away, Charlie had spent most of his time working on the new songs for his album, the one that would follow up the Beatles' White Album and strike the spark for Helter Skelter. They were message songs, like the Beatles', with lots of subtle symbols aimed at the different parts of society that would be involved in what was coming. They were the "plan" which the Beatles were asking Charlie to reveal in "Revolution 1."

Terry Melcher was the one that Manson had decided should produce this special album. According to his version of events, Terry went so far as to promise to come out and hear the new music one evening. The girls spent the whole day preparing food and joints, fixing up the house in Canoga Park where the Family was spending the winter. Melcher never showed up.

Once again Terry Melcher had failed Charlie. More than ever, Terry Melcher—in his house at the top of Cielo Drive, with his power and his money—was the focus for the bitterness and sense of betrayal that the Family felt for all those phony Hollywood hippies who kept silencing the truth Charlie had to share. These "beautiful people," Terry and all the others, were really no different from the rich piggies in their white shirts and ties and suits. And just like them, they too deserved a "damn good whacking."

Piggies

There was a lot of confusion in those first weeks in March when I returned to the Family, and not all of it was inside my head. I didn't know what to think of this new teaching of Charlie's. It seemed to make sense, especially with everybody parroting it and working so hard getting ready for what was coming, but a part of me held back. I wasn't quite sure. Meanwhile, George Spahn was telling Charlie he'd have to get us all off the ranch. The police had come up several times since the Helter Skelter Club opened, pestering George about operating a nightclub without a license. There were constantly new people coming and going, guys like Danny DeCarlo, one of the Straight Satans bikers who needed to get away from his "red freak" (barbiturate addict) wife in Venice. DeCarlo hung around mainly because he enjoyed making love with Charlie's "sweeties," as he called them, and later, during the investigation of the murders, he would be a major source of information for the prosecution.

Once George started getting uptight, Charlie decided Squeaky should talk the old man into signing over his ranch to the Family. Although nothing specific was said about it at the time, I don't think Charlie planned for him to last very long after he made out his new will. But Spahn was as stubborn as he was old, and after George made us close down the club Charlie decided we should move back to the Canoga Park house on Gresham Street.

It was more than just a house. There was a large garage in back, along with some run-down stables for working on the dune buggies and bikes, and there was also a large attic where we put all the mattresses and continued our lovemaking in the dust and cobwebs. Between working on the vehicles and getting together supplies and trying to find a secret route up through Devil's Canyon into the desert (the Canyon started just across the highway from Spahn and Charlie was convinced that the song "Helter Skelter" gave coded directions for a way through it into Death Valley), we were kept pretty busy, but Charlie wasn't comfortable down in the middle of the Valley. There were too many people. When he found out about a house up in the hills above Malibu Canyon that had been leased by the rock group Iron Butterfly but was now standing vacant, he decided we should live up there. So once more we piled everything together and made a move. Just as he had left Brooks Poston and Juanita up at Barker Ranch in the desert, however, and Squeaky at Spahn Ranch with old George, Charlie had a couple of the girls stay behind at Gresham Street, too. He liked to have lots of options.

At the Malibu Canyon house we spent most of our time roaring up and down the Santa Monica mountains in the dune buggies or trying to accommodate Charlie's constantly changing whims — like turning one of the trucks into a mobile pit stop for the dune buggies or painting the name of a fictitious movie company on all the vehicles for cover. Then, without warning sometime early in April, Charlie decided we should move back to Spahn, whether George liked it or not. The time for Helter Skelter was very close and we needed a clear escape route to the desert.

Through most of this I had still not been absolutely certain whether or not I believed everything Charlie was teaching us about the coming Apocalypse, and even though I considered myself back in the Family, I made occasional trips to Hollywood to visit Luella and get acid from her. One afternoon late in March, I took Mary Brunner and another one of the girls with me to Luella's apartment and when we got there, Luella was having a little acid party. What we were offered was a special acid I'd never dropped before called "Orange Sunshine" — and when it started coming on, it came on heavy. Suddenly another song on the White Album made sense: "...everybody's got something to hide, except me and my monkey." We were the monkeys, we realized, just bright-eyed, free little animals, totally uninhibited. The three of us started bouncing around the apartment, throwing food against the walls and laughing hysterically. As far as we could tell, we were all love-spontaneous, childlike love — even though everybody else at the party seemed turned off by us, a little frightened at our pupils so dilated that there was no more color to our eyes, just huge black holes in the middle of the white. Somehow Luella got us out of the apartment, and on the way downstairs I remember stopping to speak to one of the neighbors we'd dealt dope with in the past.

"I treat you as I treat myself," I remember saying to him solemnly, and somehow it was like a benediction, as though I was making him my brother, giving him title to all my drug business and Luella and everything of mine that was still in the apartment upstairs. "I treat you as I treat myself," I repeated and it was like the closing of a chapter. The two girls and I ran out onto the street, chattering like little apes.

As we walked down the street, the blazing light burst into our brains through totally dilated eyes that held back nothing. We were certain we were invisible. We hitched a ride over Laurel Canyon into the Valley and though I can't explain it now, the young guy who'd given us the ride suddenly jerked to attention as if he hadn't even been aware of us with him all the way over the hills. "Who are you?" he screamed. "What're you doing in my car? Where'd you come from?" As we tumbled out onto Ventura Boulevard we realized we'd been right — the boy had never seen us at all until it was time for us to get out. It was true, what Charlie had sometimes said — if you burn every thought out of your head, then there's nothing left for anyone to see.

As we walked west on Ventura Boulevard, facing the setting sun, looking directly into the orange ball of flame, it felt as though I was being magnetized by the sun itself. The sun was God, and the closer the sun came to setting, the closer the end of the world must be. All the cars going back and forth on the street suddenly seemed to be in total confusion, crashing and smashing into each other in their frantic rush to escape, but the sun just kept slowly sinking, taking no notice of them, pulling down the curtain on the world. Charlie was right, I realized; everything he said was true; I was seeing it. The Apocalypse was at hand and the present world was dying. As we passed two little children playing on the sidewalk, I suddenly ran over and scooped them up into my arms, dashing to hide them under a bush. I wanted to save them from the Helter Skelter that was coming; I wanted to protect them. There was no longer a trace of doubt in my mind. It was coming down fast, just as Charlie said, just as the Beatles said, just as the Bible said. It was coming down fast; yes it was!

On April 23, 1969, I was arrested in Van Nuys for being under the influence of drugs in public. It began with a small piece of belladonna root that Brenda-Nancy had found in the fields behind the ranch and boiled up in the kitchen, a piece no more than half an inch long and a quarter of an inch across. It ended up with me slithering across a sidewalk on my hands and knees through a crowd of schoolchildren, unable to walk, unable to make any noise except little mechanical sounds, over and over: "Beep, beep . . . beep, beep, beep." Before it was over, ten days later, I would have seen space people beeping back at me, landing and taking off from circles of light; I would have seen the wind itself. The arrest was not only the source of a mug shot that showed me grinning up at the camera like some sort of demented animal—a photograph that later became the best-known image of me in the press. It also resulted in my being fingerprinted for the first time in my life. Later it was one of those fingerprints that matched a print lifted from the freshly washed door at 10050 Cielo Drive the day after the first murders.

Even before I came back to the Family in March, Charlie had mentioned to Paul Watkins that it was beginning to look like blackie was so stupid that somebody would have to show him how to start Helter Skelter. Once we moved back to the ranch in late April, it became more and more clear who that somebody would have to be.

Ever since I'd known him, Charlie had talked about death, but it was usually spiritual death he urged upon us: death to the ego. Now there was nothing spiritual or psychological about the dying which Charlie seemed more and more obsessed with. It was violent death, physical death that he meant when he told us that death was beautiful, because it was the thing people feared the most. Yet, he said, death was nothing but an illusion in the mind anyway, so killing a human being was merely destroying a fantasy. He kept repeating that the spirit, the soul, can never be killed; it is one and eternal — the illusion of physical death merely opens the resistant spirit to realization of its essential oneness with all that is.

He became more and more interested in weapons and we began to develop quite an arsenal: rifles, pistols, knives, even a machine gun. Charlie was especially fond of a Buntline Special, Hi Standard .22 caliber Longhorn revolver he'd been given by Randy Starr, an old rodeo performer who hung around the ranch. (Quite literally "hung" — his favorite stunt was a macabre fake garroting where he'd dangle from his own specially made scaffold, eyes bulging, tongue protruding. Charlie loved it!) Besides the weapons there was the steadily growing collection of dune buggies, including Charlie's command vehicle which he covered with hanks of hair donated by all the Family members.

There was a lot more talk about fear. The purpose of fear, Charlie said, was to get rid of all thought; if you were really afraid, you were conscious of nothing but the moment and the present situation. That was being in the now and that was true clarity, true awareness. None of this was new. Charlie had often said we should live in constant fear, like wild animals always on the alert, but now the fear games developed a new edge. At Charlie's direction we'd take the tricky turns of the Santa Susana Pass at ninety to a hundred miles an hour in our dune buggies, defying centrifugal force. At night, he started sending the girls out on what he called "creepy-crawls" — slipping into darkened houses while the owners were sleeping and crawling through them, rearranging things. Although it might seem that this kind of game was designed to frighten the people who woke up the next morning and found that things had been subtly shifted in the night, the real purpose was to make the girls doing the crawling face their fear and go beyond it. Sometimes Charlie would gather us all together in the ranch house and have us imagine a rich piggie sitting in a chair in the middle of the circle we'd form. "Imagine we just yanked this pig out of his big car and stuck him here," Charlie would instruct us. Then we would project all our own fear on that piggie while we fantasized his own fear as he was surrounded by our silent staring power. Charlie would direct us until we'd actually see ourselves scaring this imaginary pig to death just by the force of what we were projecting onto him.

During this kind of game we'd usually drop acid, and after a while Charlie got in the habit of quietly talking about things that might happen, things that could be done to this imaginary piggy — things like tying him up, stabbing him, going into his house and murdering all his family and getting all his money, or frightening him into willing everything he had to us and then killing him. We'd all follow Charlie's lead and imagine the butchery and the terror, and even though it was all just a game, the images stayed locked in our brains after the game was over.

Charlie never gave up using the acid and his teaching to break down our egos and completely dominate us. He continued all the old preaching, telling us we had to cease to exist, asking us to make the gift of our love and submission to him complete. It went on day and night until finally it seemed there was so little left of me that it was pointless to even carry the empty symbols of a separate identity around with me any longer. I went out to the dump behind the ranch house and threw away everything in my wallet: driver's license, draft card, everything. Now even the fiction of there being a separate Charles Denton Watson had been destroyed, at least for me. There was just a body named Tex that carried around a little part of the all, a little part of Charlie under the illusion of self.

Not all of Charlie's attempts to condition us to fear and violence were immediate successes. The first time he told me to slip up to a house and find out what was going on inside, I just walked up and rang the doorbell, ready to ask whoever answered what he was doing. There was nobody home, but Charlie still wouldn't talk to me for a while after that.

We began stealing anything we could get our hands on: money, credit cards, traveler's checks, dune-buggie parts. It was all for Helter Skelter, Charlie told us; we had to be ready. We creepy-crawled a couple of houses in Malibu and walked off with clothes and some tape equipment that turned out to have already been stolen from NBC.

I think it was sometime in June that Charlie started saying that if blackie didn't make his move soon, we might have to start Helter Skelter for him. We all listened and agreed and added it to the doctrine, but I didn't really think the time would come when we would be killing people. It was strange, but even though I truly believed that Charlie knew everything, I could sometimes ignore what he said, even disobey him. There was the matter of speed, for instance. Charlie, for all his use of acid, was absolutely against speed. He believed it was bad for your body. But when a young guy from one of the neighboring ranches began sneaking it over, Susan-Sadie, and Bruce Davis, and I started carrying it around in the bottom of a cigarette package. Later we hid it in a Gerbers' baby-food jar under the porch of one of the buildings. I liked the way speed worked. You'd stick your finger in, sniff it up each nostril, and everything came to life. Sometimes time moved past you so fast you could barely keep up with it. Even after the murders, when I was up in the desert, I tried to get Bruce to find our little baby-food jar of speed, but somehow it had disappeared. I was willing to kill for Manson, but I wasn't willing to give up my speed.

As the summer got longer and hotter, the piggies in the fear games and the visions Charlie put in our heads for them got more and more specific.

About two miles down the hill from the ranch there was an ostentatious new suburban development with homes that managed to resemble mausoleums in their conspicuous consumption and attempted grandeur. Gradually the pig in our fantasies became one of the people from this development. Charlie began to talk about going in and taking over one of those enormous houses. As he sketched it out, we could just barge in when we were all on acid and scare the owners to death by the fear we would project onto them. Then we'd take charge of the place and live there, and the girls would pretend to be maids and keep up appearances while we ripped off everything we could for Helter Skelter. It says something about how unrealistic Charlie's visions were that he apparently believed we could really get away with something like this, that the girls could somehow convince friends and employers and neighbors that our victims were away on vacation while we cashed their checks, used their credit cards, and sold off their possessions. I don't remember exactly when or how we crossed the line between imagination and reality, but one afternoon Charlie actually went up to one of those houses while others of us waited in the car. He tried first the front door, then the back, but there was nobody home and we never got inside. Whoever lived (perhaps still lives) in that house never knew how close they came to being Manson's first victims.

When the residential development didn't seem to work out, Charlie turned his eye to the top of the hill above us — where a restaurant and gambling club overlooked the Simi Valley beyond the pass. Charlie's first idea was to rob the casino itself, but after a week of casing the place with binoculars and nighttime creepy-crawls around the grounds, he gave up on that and decided we would kidnap one of the rich customers. From there we'd follow our plans for the Chatsworth mansion: take over the pig's house and put his money into buying dune buggies and supplies for our escape to the desert. By this time, Charlie had another idea as well. Instead of scaring our victims to death, he wanted to build a jail in the sewers for them, a jail where he would be the warden-a fair switch after his seventeen years in the pigs' joint. He went so far on this one as to equip our big truck with a shortwave radio (it was supposed to block the front entrance to our subterranean prison), but then an ex-convict friend of his stole the whole rig and ran off to Texas with one of the girls.

That disappointment didn't make Manson give up on getting some of the casino patrons. He just went back to his original plan of either making them prisoners in their own home or killing them. Sometimes he'd even talk about bringing them back to the ranch and putting them in the middle of our circle so we'd have a real piggie to work on. But whatever the details, the intent was always the same: getting money for Helter Skelter.

As farfetched as it sounds, Charlie's second plan almost killed two women. One night he and I were waiting in the parking lot of the casino, looking for the right victims, when two elderly ladies came out to their car, one of them crippled. As they got in slowly, oblivious to what was happening ahead of them, Charlie pulled up to block their exit and sent me with a knife to force them into our car. I crept forward slowly, then suddenly appeared at their window, flashing my blade. The woman who was driving accelerated violently, nearly running me down as she swung around our car and took off down the driveway. We spent about fifteen minutes chasing them all over the north end of the Valley before they finally lost us somewhere near Topanga Canyon Boulevard. Once again Charlie had been cheated out of his pig. Once more his preparations for the end were frustrated. But he had gained something. He had seen that at least one of his Family had reached the point that he would try to do anything Charlie asked, even try to kill.

Considering all Charlie's plans, it is ironic that the first person he actually killed (or thought he killed) was not a rich establishment pig at all, but rather a black man, a dope dealer in Hollywood.

You Were Only Waiting for This Moment

Sometime late in June, having failed to raise any funds for Helter Skelter by kidnapping piggies, Charlie decided I should ask Luella for money. I called her but she refused.

That wasn't good enough for Charlie: I should figure out a way to get some cash out of her, he said. I thought awhile and came up with an idea. Since grass was particularly scarce at the time, I called Luella back on July 1 and said that the Family had $100 and wanted to buy a kilo of grass, but our Mafia vending-machine connection would only sell 25 kilos at a throw, for a cool $2,500. I tried to be casual in planting the seed, certain that a chance to score two dozen kilos of grass at a time like this would be more than Luella could resist. I was right. She called back about half an hour later and told me that she knew somebody who was interested in buying the extra kilos, but she needed to make some money out of the deal as well.

Over the phone we worked out an arrangement where we'd pay my supposed connection $2,500 for the 25 kilos, but charge Luella's client $125 apiece. That way, I would get three kilos free, the client would get twenty-two kilos, and Luella would make herself a profit of a couple of hundred dollars. There was one condition, I insisted — my connection didn't want to deal with anyone but me. Luella agreed. Her friend would front the money; she and I would go for the grass and then bring it back to him at her apartment. I couldn't believe it was working out so easily — T. J. would drive me down to L.A. and drop me near Luella's apartment to make it look like I'd hitchhiked. He'd then go on to the dealer's place on the other side of town, parking in back of the apartment house out of which the man worked. Luella would drive me there with the money, and I'd go in the front door and out the back with the bread, leaving her to explain things to her friend.

The fact that I was badly "burning" a woman I'd once loved never really sank in — it was for Charlie and for Helter Skelter — and besides, there was no right or wrong anyway, only what had to be.

When I got to Luella's apartment, however, there was a snag. Her friend, a black dealer named Bernard Crowe — "Big Crow" or "Lotsapoppa" in the trade — wasn't about to just hand over $2,750 to me on the promise that I'd bring him back some grass. While he and one of his boys waited downstairs in their big black Caddy, another one of his men tried to talk Luella and me into letting them come with us. I tried everything I could think of, including walking out the door, but finally we ended up riding out to the connection's apartment in Crowe's big black car, with his men on either side of us, just like something out of a movie.

I'd made Crowe's man promise that once we got to the apartment they'd all wait in the car — since, I claimed, my connection was very nervous about being burned off — but when we got there they insisted they were coming in with me. Luella recognized the building and tried to convince them that everything was on the level, but I just said, "Okay, this is where it ends; let's go back to Hollywood."

It was like a game of poker, each side not trusting the other and bluffing for everything we were worth. Finally they agreed I could go in alone. They would keep Luella in the car as a guarantee that I would bring them the grass. When Crowe threatened violence to her if I tried to cheat them, I gave him one of my Texas grins and drawled that they should know I'd be coming back when they had my girl. I don't remember whether I really thought they would hurt her or not — there was no reason not to believe he meant what he said — but it didn't much matter to me what they did to Luella, as long as I got the money for Charlie. They gave me the cash and I went straight into the front of the apartment and straight out the back and T. J. and I were off to the ranch.

We were still showing the money to Charlie when the phone rang. It was Luella and Big Crow, not surprisingly, raging mad. We'd already agreed that Charlie would handle this end of it, and I listened as he claimed that I'd left the Family several weeks before and that he didn't know anything about where I'd gone. It didn't sell. Charlie told us when he hung up that Big Crow said he knew I was at the ranch and if he didn't get back his money he was coming out with his boys and killing everyone at Spahn. Charlie believed him. He sent Sadie and me up into the hills with a sleeping bag and said he would deal with Crowe.

I heard the rest of what happened from T. J. the next day. He and Charlie drove into Hollywood to the apartment where Big Crow lived. Charlie took Randy Starr's .22 Buntline revolver with him and tucked it into the back of his pants. At a signal from him, T. J., who would be standing behind Charlie, was supposed to take the gun and kill the black man. But once they got inside, T. J. couldn't do it; he just stood behind Charlie, frozen. After a few minutes of verbal baiting back and forth, Charlie whipped out the pistol, pointed it at the towering black man and pulled the trigger.

Nothing happened but a click. Charlie tried again. Still just a click. Big Crow's white sidekicks started to snicker. Another click. Finally Crowe stood up, grinning: "You crazy! You come at me with an empty . . . ." Then the gun went off and Crowe went down, bleeding in the chest-dying, T. J. said. (The next thing Charlie did was turn the gun on one of the dudes who was wearing a fancy buckskin fringed jacket and demand he give it to him. When Manson was arrested months later at Barker Ranch on suspicion of "grand theft auto," he was wearing that buckskin jacket.)

At the ranch the next day, Charlie couldn't stop talking about how he "plugged blackie." We all assumed Crowe had died, especially when a report came on the news that the body of a Black Panther had been dumped near U.C.L.A. the night before. This made us a little uneasy, since we hadn't figured on getting involved with the Panthers, and Charlie got even more nervous when almost immediately it seemed that all kinds of blacks started showing up, renting horses. He was convinced they were Panther spies and he started posting armed guards at night and having us sleep scattered back in the hills. If we'd needed any more proof that Helter Skelter was coming down very soon, this was it—blackie was trying to get at the chosen ones.

Much later I learned that Bernard Crowe — who in fact never had anything to do with the Panthers — had not been killed, only wounded. His friends had taken him away and had lain low, fearful that if Charlie found out the Big Crow was still alive he might come after him again. He might have, but I doubt it, because very soon Charlie would have bigger fish to fry. Much bigger.

Three days after this first blood, someone important was added to the Family. On July 4, Gypsy brought a quiet, blond hippie named Linda Kasabian and her little girl, Tanya, back with her from a visit to some people we knew in Topanga. Linda joined the Family that same day, without even meeting Charlie, and that night I introduced her to our truth. Linda later said that when we made love it was like being possessed. For me it was a more complete sensation of oneness than I'd ever known with a woman — it was as if our two bodies literally became one and it was no longer possible to feel where I ended and she began. Linda and I talked very late that night, just the two of us in a little room in the ranch house. I told her she should steal some money that the man she'd been staying with had inherited, and when she protested that she couldn't do that, since he was a good friend who trusted her, I quoted Charlie and told her that there was no wrong, no sin; everything anyone had was meant to be shared. Linda had already given the Family whatever she owned and the next day she went back to Topanga and returned a little while later with $5,000 she'd ripped off according to my instructions. A little over a month later, simply because she was about the only Family member with a valid driver's license, newcomer Linda Kasabian would be sent out in the middle of the night to Terry Melcher's old house at 10050 Cielo Drive with Sadie and Katie and me — and very clear instructions from Charlie Manson.

That July was a crazy time. We got more and more paranoid about the blacks that kept appearing. We spent our nights patrolling the ranch, sleeping in shifts, with guns and firebombs ready. During the day we worked on the new dune buggies and trucks we bought with Linda's money and what I'd stolen from Crowe. It still wasn't enough for Charlie's plans, so one day Mary Brunner went into town and drove back to the ranch in a brand-new 1969 VW she'd stolen off a dealer's lot. We stripped everything we thought we could use out of it and rolled the shell down one of the ravines behind the ranch house.

We also made a number of trips down to an army-surplus store in the Valley for supplies and weapons, especially knives, and it was at this point that we bought the Buck knives and the chrome-plated bayonet, later put to such hideous use. On the first of these trips, while we were carrying all of Linda's $5,000 in crisp new $100 bills, we were pulled over by the police for a faulty taillight. When they discovered the money, Charlie and I were taken to the station and questioned separately. We told the officers, quite honestly as far as it went, that the money had been given to us, and eventually we were released. Several nights later there was a small raid on the ranch, just a few police cars, nothing like the August 16 raid, and most of us were in the hills anyway, waiting for blackie. The guards posted near the gate used our walkie-talkie system to warn the women and babies to get out, so the cops didn't find much of anyone except a few legitimate ranch hands.

From our perches in the hills, we watched the police wander through the empty sets and ranch houses, watched them shake down the people they'd hauled out of the bunkhouse in the circle of brightness their headlights made, watched the red and white lights of the police cars whirl madly in the darkness. We all knew that Charlie was on parole, and all I could think as we crouched in the darkness, taking in the light show at the ranch below us, was: "What if they find Charlie and take him away? What am I going to do without Charlie?" Finally the police cars drove off without arresting anybody, but the raid was a sign, another indication we had very little time left to get ready for what was coming.

Charlie decided we needed still more money; there weren't enough dune buggies and supplies. Over the past year, he and various other Family members had spent time with a young musician and teacher in Topanga Canyon named Gary Hinman. Now Charlie somehow had an idea that Hinman had recently come into some money, so one Friday late in July (I later found out it was July 25) he called together Mary and Sadie and a boy named Bobby Beausoleil whom I'd never known very well but who'd been with Charlie on and off since I'd first come to the Family.

The rest of us could tell something was up, but all we knew at first was that the three of them were supposed to go to Hinman and lay so much fear on him that he would give us everything he had, including the money Charlie was certain he was keeping at the house.

The three of them left, and the next thing we knew there was a phone call from Bobby for Charlie. Other calls followed throughout the day, and finally sometime that night Charlie and Bruce Davis drove over to Hinman's place. Charlie took along a large sword he'd conned the Straight Satans out of earlier and when he got back all he'd say was that he'd had to "slice" Hinman to put some real fear in him.

The calls from Beausoleil continued all day Saturday and even though we kept up business as usual — helping with the horses, the girls playing at being guides—we were all on edge, waiting. Midday on Sunday there was a final call and Charlie's word was: "You know what to do."

A little while later Bobby and the two girls came back with Hinman's VW bus and Fiat. A set of bagpipes that we all knew had belonged to Gary appeared on a shelf in the kitchen, and Bobby was bursting with pride. It didn't take much imagination to figure out what had gone down. That night T. J. quietly disappeared—it was too much for him.

Eventually, I didn't have to use any imagination to know what had happened over those three days at Gary Hinman's Topanga house. Bobby bragged a lot, and Mary and Susan gradually filled in the details. On Friday the three of them paid what was supposedly a friendly call to the musician, making general conversation, just hanging around. After a while Bobby brought up Helter Skelter and then told Gary that the Family needed all his money, demanding he give it to him immediately. Gary thought he was kidding at first, but when he realized Bobby was serious he insisted he didn't have any money. At that point Bobby pulled out a small handgun and started pistol-whipping him. In the fight that followed the gun went off, but it didn't hit anyone. Finally Bobby and the girls got Gary tied up and made their first call to Spahn, asking Charlie what to do since Gary wasn't "cooperating."

Throughout the rest of the day Charlie continued to give long-distance instructions, but finally he and Bruce arrived at Hinman's late that evening. Gary pleaded with Charlie — swearing he didn't have any money, reminding him of their friendship, begging Charlie to take the others and leave. Manson said nothing, just listened silently until he suddenly raised the sword and cut Gary's left ear in half. As Gary whimpered in pain and fear, Charlie quietly ordered him to sign over everything he had to the Family or die. That was the choice. Then he and Bruce left, taking the bagpipes with them.

That night Mary, Sadie, and Bobby took turns watching Gary, sleeping in shifts, and all day Saturday Bobby badgered him, demanding to know about the money. Gary did sign over the pink slips to his bus and Fiat, but he continued to insist that he didn't have any money. After another long night of watching in turns and another pistol-whipping, Bobby gave up-apparently convinced that Hinman was telling the truth—and called Charlie, asking what to do, since he was afraid Gary would go to the police if they just left him. Manson's reply was what we had heard: "You know what to do."

Bobby stabbed Hinman several times in the chest in front of the girls, then knelt down beside him as he was dying and told him he was a pig that had no reason to live anyway, told him he should thank him for putting an end to him. After Gary died, Bobby stuck his hand in the blood and wrote POLITICAL PIGGIE on the wall and made the mark of a paw print with his palm, this to give the appearance that Black Panthers, whose symbol was a panther's paw, had killed the white musician. Whether this was a spontaneous idea of Bobby's (or something Charlie had told him to do) I'm not sure, but it meant that if Gary wouldn't (or couldn't) contribute to financing Helter Skelter, he might at least give blackie some useful ideas and put a little fear into the establishment as well.

When Bobby was finished, the three of them wiped down the walls for fingerprints (not very well, since several prints were later found), hot-wired the two vehicles and drove back to the ranch. Two days later Bobby returned to Hinman's to see if anybody had discovered the body yet. He came back gloating — word passed through the Family that he'd been able to hear the maggots crunching through Gary Hinman's bloated flesh.

Bobby left Spahn Ranch several days later — as he often did, coming and going — and on August 6 he was arrested somewhere up the coast, driving Hinman's Fiat, with the bloody murder knife still tucked in the tire well.

When word of the arrest got to the Family, Charlie disappeared for a couple of days up to Big Sur, something very unusual for him. When he got back, he called us all together. It was the afternoon of August 8, 1969, and his message was simple.

"Now is the time for Helter Skelter."

Helter Skelter I (August 8-9)

There were three basic motives behind the murders that took place sometime past midnight on August 9. The most obvious was the one Charlie had articulated to us that afternoon: to do what blackie didn't have the energy or the smarts to do — ignite Helter Skelter and bring in Charlie's kingdom. There was also the need for more cash, first of all to finance our preparations for Armageddon — the same thing that had motivated the drug burn and Bernard Crowe's supposed murder, the killing of Gary Hinman, and all the proposed abductions and murders in the Chatsworth area — and also to pay $600 bail for Mary Brunner, who had been arrested earlier that day for using a stolen Sears' credit card. If she had not been in custody, Mary would most likely have been the one sent with us that night, instead of Linda, since Mary had the other valid driver's license in the Family and had already proven herself at Gary Hinman's. Beyond getting money and bringing down Helter Skelter, there was a third, less important purpose: to clear Bobby Beausoleil of the Hinman slaying by committing a similar crime while he was in jail.

After Charlie's announcement in the afternoon, the ranch became very quiet, with an undercurrent of electric excitement, even dread. With everything that had been happening over the past weeks there was no question that we would be the ones to bring down the Apocalypse, not some black militants from Watts. The only question was which of us and how.

We ate late that night, and sometime after dinner a lot of us were in the back ranch house with our clothes off, just lying around, some people making love. Usually these times were very mellow, all of us together like animals in a nest, nuzzling and warm, bodies close, but tonight the tension of the afternoon continued, putting everyone on edge. Earlier that afternoon I'd taken some acid Charlie gave me, but by now I was coming down from it.

It all began with something I didn't see, only heard about later: Charlie sat up slowly and ran his finger across his throat. Then he told me to put on my clothes and come with him. As we walked up the hill in the darkness he said, "I've got a favor I want you to do for me tonight . . . but it'll take a lot of nerve to do it."

I told him he knew I'd do anything he wanted. He brought up the "killing" of Bernard Crowe, saying how he'd taken care of that for me when it was really my mess. Now he wanted me to take care of something for him. Again I assured him I would do whatever he asked me. He stopped and stared at me strangely, leaning against one of the cars parked around us.

"What I want . . . I want you to go to that house where Melcher used to live — (we knew that by now Terry had moved down to a beach house in Malibu) — I want you to take a couple of the girls I'll send with you and go down there . . . and totally destroy everyone in that house, as gruesome as you can. Make it a real nice murder, just as bad as you've ever seen. And get all their money."

Then he started a careful list of instructions: how we were to take some rope and good knives, how I was to cut the telephone wires before we went in and that I should take the bolt cutters off of his dune buggie to do it, how we should not use the automatic gate since it might be attached to an alarm system. He also said to wear dark colors, take a change of clothes with us, and burn those we did the killing in.

Then he laid out how he wanted the murders themselves done. He apparently didn't know who was living in the house or how many people we might find, but whoever and however many it was we were to kill them all, mutilate them ("Pull out their eyes and hang them on the mirrors!"), and write messages on the walls in their blood. When he started listing what he wanted written—things like HELTER SKELTER and RISE—I told him I couldn't remember all that. But he said it was okay; the girls would know what to write. Just before he went off to get the women, he handed me the .22 Buntline pistol he'd been given by old Randy Starr, but he said to use knives whenever possible, not the gun.

While Manson went back to the movie set to round up Sadie, Katie, and Linda, I reeled over to the porch where

Sadie and I kept our Gerbers' jar of speed hidden. Of course we'd known it was coming to this. We'd practiced so many times, in our heads, sitting around that empty chair in the ranch house, projecting scenes much like the one Charlie had just described on some imaginary piggie, and if the world was ending at any moment and if death was only a figment of the mind and if . . . and if . . . . Despite all we'd been taught, I was spinning inside, trembling. I took a couple of deep snorts of speed and went to get the clothes and rope and bolt cutters as Charlie had ordered.

Manson had told me to borrow an old yellow 1959 Ford that belonged to Johnny Swartz, one of the ranch hands, since it was the only car that was running at the time. I did, telling him we were going downtown for some music. Then somehow Charlie was back with me again, whispering in my ear that we needed money to get Mary out of jail and that "if you don't get enough money at the Melcher house, then go on to the house next door and then the house after that until you get six hundred dollars."

We piled into the car, me in the driver's seat with Sadie next to me, Katie and Linda in back, all of us in dark shirts and jeans. I was wearing cowboy boots but the girls were barefoot. There were three knives-one of them the one that Katie would end up with, with a broken handle that was taped-and Randy Starr's gun. We were ready.

As we started off, Charlie stopped us and came over to lean into the open window. "Remember to leave a sign," he told the girls, "something witchy." He waved to us as we drove off.

What took place in the next few hours will be difficult to read, even more difficult to tell. Up to now, I've tried to recapture the feelings (or lack of them) and attitudes that were mine at any given point in my story, without interjecting who and what I am today, but there is no way to tell what follows without first saying that the events of that horrible night and the one that followed it cause me more agony and grief than I could ever express. I said earlier that at the time — and in the months following these senseless, brutal crimes — I felt nothing. It is true. But one of the greatest and yet most painful gifts I've been given as I've had my self restored is the ability to realize what really took place those two nights, to feel it more deeply and completely than I could bear if it were not for another gift I've also been given. But all that comes later. That night there was only the knowledge of what had to be done, not with pleasure any more than with revulsion or regret, not with any feeling at all, just done.

We drove in silence for some time, as if we were frozen. Finally I told the girls we were going to the house where Terry Melcher used to live because I knew the place, the layout, and that when we got there we were going to kill everyone we found and get their money. I had Linda wrap up the knives and gun in a rag on the floor and hide them at her feet. If we were stopped by the police on the way, I told her, she was to throw the whole bundle out the window.

We got lost. I missed a turnoff and we ended up going all the way into Hollywood, then back west on Santa Monica Boulevard through West Hollywood and the edges of Beverly Hills. We cut up past the landscaped mansions, most of them dark now, to Sunset Boulevard, then to Benedict Canyon, then finally turned left onto Cielo Drive.

When I pulled up to the big gate at the end of the private drive, directly under a power pole, I told the girls we'd all have to be truly one, truly together to do what we had to do. I climbed onto the hood of the car and shinnied up the pole, cutting the telephone line with the bolt cutters one of the girls had handed me through the window. For some reason I had no uncertainty about which wires were which — it was as though Charlie's instructions were tape-recorded in my mind and being played back, step by step, as I needed them. After the wires had fallen, I backed the car down the driveway to the street below and parked. We gathered up our clothes and weapons and quietly slipped back up the driveway. I carried the white rope over my shoulder. When we reached the gate I peered in — you couldn't see the main house from there, only a corner of the garage (a yellow bug light was burning, so I was assured I hadn't cut any power lines by mistake) and a split-rail fence along the edge of the lawn that had colored Christmas lights glowing on it, even though it was the middle of summer.

There was a steep, brushy embankment coming down to the right side of the fence, so we tossed the extra clothes over the gate and climbed up the slope, dropping to the other side. On my first try, the speed I'd sniffed before we left threw my balance off and I ended up tumbling down to the pavement.

We had barely gotten over the gate when there was the sound of a car, and headlights loomed at the top of the driveway, heading toward us. I told the girls to get into the bushes, lie down, and be quiet. The driver of the car had to stop and roll down his window to push the button for the automatic gate, and as he did so I stepped forward out of the shadows, gun in right hand, knife in left, commanding him to halt. A terrified teenage boy looked up at me, his glasses flashing. He was Steven Parent. Much later I would learn he had been visiting a groundskeeper — William Garretson — who lived in a guest cottage behind the main house and pool, a cottage we never discovered in the rampage that followed. (It would actually be some time before I learned the names of our victims. That night and the night after, they were so many impersonal blobs to be dealt with as Charlie had instructed. To make what follows as clear as possible, however, the victims' names will be used.)

As I lunged forward the boy cried out: "Please . . . please, don't hurt me. I'm your friend . . . . I won't tell." I shot him four times and at some point struck out with the knife, slashing at the left arm he raised to shield his face. After he had slumped back across the seat I reached in the window, cutting the motor and lights before I pushed the car part of the way back up the driveway where it would be less visible from the private road.

Hissing for the girls to follow me, I started up the driveway and rounded the turn to the house. A neatly clipped lawn stretched from the porch to the edge of the terraced hillside that overlooked the shimmering lights of the whole west side of the L.A. basin. There was no sign that anyone inside had been roused by the shots.

I told Linda to go around to the back of the house and check for open doors or windows. She was back in a few moments, saying that everything was locked. A window that opened into the entry hall, just to the side of the front door, was raised several inches, so-after telling Linda to go back down to the gate and keep watch in case anyone was alerted by the sounds of the shots — I slit the bottom of the screen, removed it, pushed up the window, and climbed through. It was very still inside the house.

I crept to the front door and let in Sadie. Katie had disappeared for the moment, gone down to Linda at the gate to get her knife, so the two of us slowly moved past a couple of large blue trunks that were standing in the hallway and slipped into the living room beyond. At first it seemed empty, but as we got in farther we could see a large blond man — Voytek Frykowski — asleep on a sofa that faced into the room, away from the door, and was incongruously draped with a large American flag. As we stood over him, I whispered to Sadie to check the rest of the house.

Frykowski stirred at the sound of my voice and mumbled something like: "What time is it?" I kicked him in the head. As he struggled up in confusion, mumbling: "Who are you? What do you want?" I answered, "I'm the devil and I'm here to do the devil's business."

I jerked my head to Sadie and she disappeared down the hall. Frykowski started to say something else but I cut him off: "Another word and you're dead!" When I asked him where his money was, he nodded toward a desk, but then Katie appeared and Sadie returned from the back of the house, saying there were three others: a man and two women. I told her to get them.

She brought back Abigail Folger first, a dark-haired woman in a long white nightgown. Katie held a knife on her while Sadie went back for the other two. When she looked helplessly to Frykowski he shook his head slightly and she said nothing.

Sadie returned with the other man, Jay Sebring, and a blond woman in bra and panties with a negligee thrown around her shoulders. She was Sharon Tate. Somehow I didn't notice she was in the last stages of pregnancy.

One of the many effects of speed is to make the intention or thought of an action and that action itself almost inseparable, as if you leap ahead in time and experience your next move before you actually make it. There in that living room on the hill, with Charlie's instructions ticking through my brain, it was as if time telescoped, until one act tripped over the next in sudden bursts of blinding color and motion.

Sharon hesitated at the entrance to the living room, and I leapt forward and grabbed her arm, jerking her in after Sadie and Sebring while I flipped off the hall light with my elbow. (Avoid fingerprints, my mind had clicked.) When Sebring turned back, protesting my roughness, I told him, as I had Frykowski, that if he said one more word he would die. "He means it," Frykowski warned from the sofa.

I had already tied Frykowski's hands behind him with one end of the rope we'd brought and now I dragged the rope over to Sebring and tied him, while Sadie tied a towel around Frykowski's wrists according to my instructions. I wrapped the rope around Sebring's neck and then slung it up over one of the rafters that ran across the room and supported a loft above the fireplace. When I started to tie the rope around Sharon's neck, Sebring struggled forward in the chair he was seated in beside the fireplace, shouting for me to be careful of her.

"I told you, 'One more word and you're dead,' " I screamed and shot him. As he slumped forward onto the rug, still alive, Sharon became hysterical, but the Folger woman seemed anxious to cooperate, as if somehow she could bring sanity into the madness simply by maintaining her own control.

"I want all the money you've got here," I barked, and Abigail took Sadie into her bedroom and gave her the money in her wallet. When they came back with only seventy dollars, I shouted: "You mean that's all you've got?"

"How much do you want?" Frykowski asked.

"We want thousands!"

Sharon had pulled herself together enough to say that they didn't have any more money in the house but that they could get us some if we'd give them time. "You know I'm not kidding," I asked, and she murmured, "Yes, I know."

Sebring was breathing hard, groaning, and in the sudden silence I didn't know what else to do — I went over to him and stabbed him until I thought he was dead.

The women began to scream and someone asked, "What are you going to do with us?"

"You're all going to die," I answered.

They began pleading with us for their lives, and suddenly Frykowski started kicking and fighting, jerking at the towel that bound his hands. "Kill him!" I ordered Sadie, but he dragged her down as she flailed at him awkwardly with the knife, stabbing him in the legs several times. Then she had lost the knife in the cushions and Frykowski was loose, tearing her hair and pulling her down onto the floor. I would have shot him, but he and Sadie kept rolling and fighting, so I finally threw myself on him and beat him over the head with the butt of the gun until it broke, a section of the grip dropping to the floor. He was enormously powerful, fighting for his life as he dragged the two of us across the hall toward the front door, knocking over the trunks.

As we staggered out onto the front porch, he kept screaming, "Help me. o God, help me!" I stabbed him over and over, blindly, the whole world spinning and turning as red as the blood that was smearing and spattering everywhere. Finally I shot him twice and he slumped onto the stone porch. I looked up and realized Linda was standing on the walk, staring at me in horror. She must have been there when we first came out, as well, since I could suddenly remember her screaming to Sadie, "Make it stop!" and Sadie shrieking back that it was too late.

As Frykowski sank down on the flagstones, Sadie yelled that someone was getting away. I looked across the lawn and saw Abigail Folger dashing toward the fence with Katie behind her, knife raised. Blood was already streaking the white nightgown.

I ran across the grass as Katie tackled her. Suddenly she stopped fighting. Looking up at me as she lay on her back, she whispered without emotion, "I give up; you've got me." It was as if my hand and the knife were one, plunging up and down. I felt nothing.

Then I realized that Frykowski had somehow managed to drag himself off the porch and was struggling across the lawn. I ran back to him, and once more the mechanical knife that was my arm drove down, again and again, until my wrist disappeared in the mess.

Finally I stood up and went back inside with Katie. Sadie was sitting next to Sharon on the couch as the pathetic blond woman sobbed, begging us to take her with us and let her have her baby before we killed her. It was the first time I'd realized she was pregnant, and for a moment it almost seemed like a good idea. But then Katie hissed, "Kill her!" and Charlie's tape whirred, "Kill her!" inside my head and I looked at Sadie. But she just sat there holding Sharon, so I reached out and made the first cut across her cheek. Later, Prosecutor Bugliosi — because of some things Susan-Sadie bragged about in jail in one of her attempts to get attention-was convinced that it was she who killed Sharon Tate, but his suspicion was not true. It was my hand that struck out, over and over, until the cries of "Mother . . . mother . . ." stopped. Suddenly it seemed very quiet. It was over.

We found ourselves whispering. "Are they all dead?" I asked. "Yes," Sadie replied. As we started to leave I remembered Charlie's last order. "Write something," I told Sadie. "Write something that will shock the world." She grabbed the towel that had bound Frykowski's hands and disappeared behind the sofa. A moment later she stepped out to the porch and wrote the letters P-I-G on the front door in blood.

Then we were running down the driveway. Linda was gone, so I jammed my finger down on the automatic gate button, leaving a bloody fingerprint that would have been useful evidence if a policeman hadn't obliterated it the next day.

We found Linda at the car, with the engine already started. Katie had grabbed our extra clothes from the bushes, and we all tumbled in — Linda squealing away, while in the front seat next to her I ripped off the blood-sopped black turtleneck I'd been wearing. As we hurried away, I suddenly remembered that Charlie had told us to go on to other houses until we had $600. But we were already heading out and I felt as though I didn't have the strength to do anything but drive back to the ranch.

We were all talking at once. Linda asked about the broken gun grip, and I told her I'd cracked it on the big guy's head. I lashed out at Sadie for losing her knife. Katie kept complaining that her hand hurt — her knife hadn't had a proper handle and she'd kept hitting bones when she struck.

Linda turned off Benedict Canyon onto Portola Drive, one of the winding side streets, looking for a place where we could wash. Finally we saw an exposed hose. As we poured the water over ourselves, drenching our hair and clothes, a man and woman suddenly appeared at their door in bathrobes, asking us what we were doing.

I put on my Texas accent, saying we had just been walking and needed a drink. As we ran back to the car, the man followed us, his wife shrieking, "Get the license number; get the number!" from the doorway. In my rush I flooded the engine, and as I struggled to get the car started again the old man came up to my window and stuck his hand in, grabbing for the keys. I managed to crank up the glass and drive off, leaving him shouting after us in the middle of the road. For some reason it never occurred to any of us to try to kill him — he didn't live on Cielo Drive.

We tossed the clothes over an embankment off Mulholland Drive, a winding road on the crest of the hills between the city and the Valley, and Linda threw out the knives one by one as we rode along (one bounced off the curb into the middle of the street and we had to stop and throw it into a ravine). I flung the gun away myself, with my left hand while I was driving. Once we got down into the Valley we stopped for gas (we paid for it out of the seventy dollars we stole from Abigail Folger) and took turns going into the rest rooms to check for blood spots. Linda drove the rest of the way home.

Charlie was waiting for us on the boardwalk of the old movie set, dancing around naked with Nancy Pitman (Brenda McCann) in the moonlight. His first words were: "What're you doing home so early?"

I told him what had happened — it had been messy, like he wanted, lots of panic, everybody dead. Sadie told him my line about the devil, and he grinned, pleased. When he asked why we didn't go to any other houses I just shrugged. Then he looked each of us in the eye solemnly.

"Do you have any remorse?" he demanded.

"No," we each replied.

"Okay," he said gently. "Go to sleep and don't tell anyone." As the girls wandered off, he called me back.

"Was it really Helter Skelter?" he asked.

"Yeah, it was sure Helter Skelter."

Helter Skelter II (August 9-10)

I slept very late Saturday, then spent part of the afternoon working on dune buggies and snorting speed with Bruce Davis. At some point during the day Sadie told me that our murders were on the news and that we'd killed some really "beautiful people," but the names didn't mean anything to me and I immediately forgot most of them except Sharon Tate. I did listen to a few radio broadcasts later in the afternoon, but when the Family members who were in the know gathered around a television up at the house for the six o'clock news, I stayed away. I didn't even get together with them later in the evening when Charlie broke out the grass and they all sang. I didn't really feel anything for what had happened, for what I'd done — but I needed to be by myself.

Then it was night and Charlie called us together again — Linda, Katie, Sadie, and me. And two more as well: mentally defective Clem and Leslie, the little mountain-folk girl who was so easy for the others to push around. It would be the same as last night, he told us, only tonight we'd get two separate houses instead of just one. And this time we'd do it right. There'd been too much panic at the Tate house; the girls had told him what had gone down. Tonight would be different. Tonight he would show us how to do it.

We all put on dark clothing again, except Clem who wore a khaki jacket, and before we left, Charlie gave me a light tab of acid. While people were getting things together, Sadie and I took the opportunity to hit our speed bottle and I gave myself three good snorts in each nostril. I knew now I'd need it for what was to come. When we were all gathered at the car, Charlie handed me a .45 automatic pistol. He also had the chrome-plated bayonet we'd bought at the army-surplus store at the same time we'd purchased the Buck knives used at the Tate house. Linda and I got in the front seat with Charlie, and the four others piled in back.

We ended up driving for about three hours. Sometimes Charlie would be at the wheel, sometimes Linda, with Charlie giving her directions. Between the speed and the acid, I wasn't always certain exactly where we were. Somehow we managed to get from Pasadena to the beach to Hollywood, with several stops along the way. There wasn't much conversation as we drove, except for Charlie's asking Sadie a few details about the night before — if we'd been careful not to leave prints, how she lost her knife, what had been written on the walls.

Our first stop was somewhere in Pasadena. We'd driven slowly through several neighborhoods before Charlie and I finally walked up to a house and peered in the windows. In the living room, bathed in warm light, we could see framed photographs of children arranged neatly on one wall. Charlie shook his head, and when we were back at the car he told us he didn't want to kill children, not yet — but the time might come, he warned, when we'd have to kill the children as well. A few minutes later another house — a mansion on top of a hill — was rejected because the neighboring homes were too close to it. Charlie said that someone might hear screams.

Before Charlie settled on the house on Waverly Drive, he would consider three more murders and attempt one of them. Somewhere in Pasadena he stopped at a church and left us in the car, saying he was going to kill the priest. He returned after a few moments and told us everything was locked up and no one had answered the rectory bell. In another residential neighborhood, we saw a couple pulling into their driveway. Charlie stopped across the street, but after waiting for a few minutes he changed his mind and we headed out to the beach. An hour later, coming toward town on Sunset Boulevard, we passed a small white sports car. Linda was driving at this point, and Charlie told her to pull up beside the car at the next signal — he was going to kill the driver. She did what she was told and he jumped out, the gun in his hand. But just then the light turned green and the sports car took off, the driver never aware how close he had come to death.

After that, Charlie started giving very specific directions to Linda, as if he had a particular place in mind. Eventually we ended up parked across the street from a large old Spanish-style house at 3301 Waverly Drive, near Griffith Park in the Los Feliz section of town. Apparently Linda recognized a house nearby, because she said something to Charlie about not hitting it.

Charlie also knew the other place, having been there for an acid party with some of the Family over a year before, but he told her no, it was this house, the one directly across from us with the boat in the driveway—this was the house where Helter Skelter would fall again.

Telling us to wait, Charlie slipped up to the house alone. A few minutes later he was back, telling me to come with him. Pointing through one of the windows, he showed me a man asleep on a couch with a newspaper over his face. We went in the unlocked back door and, as a big dog nosed at us with friendly curiosity, crossed through the kitchen into the living room, Charlie still carrying the gun, me with the bayonet.

Charlie poked the man gently with the pistol to wake him up. As with Voytek Frykowski the night before, grocery-store owner Leno LaBianca's first words were: "Who are you? What do you want?"

Holding the gun on him, Charlie smiled and murmured, "We're not going to hurt you. Just relax. Don't be afraid."

"How can I help being afraid when you've got a gun on me?" LaBianca asked with unintentional irony.

Charlie's voice remained low, soothing: "It's okay; I'm your friend. We don't want anything but money."

Telling the heavyset man to roll over onto his stomach, Charlie pulled off a leather thong that had been looped around his neck and had me tie LaBianca's hands with it. I must have cinched him up pretty firmly, because he immediately protested that it was too tight, especially when we turned him onto his back again with the weight of his body pressing down on his wrists.

Charlie asked if there was anyone else in the house. Yes, LaBianca answered, his wife was in the bedroom. Charlie disappeared for a minute or two and then returned with Rosemary LaBianca, holding the gun on her but still murmuring assurances that no one was going to be hurt, this was just a simple robbery. He sat the frightened-looking woman at her husband's feet. LaBianca had on pajamas, and I later found out that his wife had pulled the blue dress she was now wearing over her pink nightgown after Charlie had suddenly appeared in her bedroom.

Mr. LaBianca was still complaining that his hands were bound too tightly, and Mrs. LaBianca turned to Charlie and said, "You're hurting my husband . . . the way he's sitting. Can't you get him in a more comfortable position?" But LaBianca stayed as he was. Soon after his wife was brought into the room he turned to Charlie with an attempt at reason: "Look, we'll give you anything you want; just tell us."

Charlie, still speaking with almost hypnotic calm, answered, "Do you have any cash?" LaBianca told him that the only cash in the house was what he'd left on his nightstand next to the bed and perhaps a little in his wife's wallet. Charlie sent me for both and was obviously displeased at how little money there was. "I can get you more," LaBianca insisted nervously. "Just let me take you to my store and you can get as much as you want."

"No," Charlie answered, "we just want what's here." Then he decided to separate them again.

We took Mrs. LaBianca back to the bedroom and stripped off the pillowcases. Following Charlie's instructions to gag them, I went into the living room, put a pillowcase over Leno LaBianca's head and tied a lamp cord around his skull and through his mouth as tightly as I could. Then I went back into the bedroom and did the same with Mrs. LaBianca, telling her not to make a sound because we would be right in the next room.

Charlie left at this point, taking the gun and the wallet with him. His last words were: "Make sure the girls get to do some of it, both of them." A minute or two later, Katie and Leslie appeared in the kitchen, holding their changes of clothing.

I thought I was whispering when I asked, "Did he say to kill them?" — but perhaps my voice was louder than I thought, because as they nodded grimly, Leno LaBianca began to scream from the living room, "You're going to kill us, aren't you? You're going to kill us!" I somehow knew from the look on her face that Leslie didn't want to go through with what was coming, but like all the rest of us, she must have felt she owed it to Charlie to do whatever he asked, since he'd given himself so totally for us. Katie, on the other hand, began to look through the kitchen drawers for knives with positive relish.

Mr. LaBianca continued to shout. I remember being surprised that he could talk so much with the wire and pillow material in his mouth. As the girls ran to the bedroom on my instructions, I walked back to the sofa with the bayonet and the horror began all over again. I drove the chrome-plated blade down full force. "Don't stab me anymore," he managed to scream, even though the first thrust had been through his throat. "I'm dead, I'm dead . . . ." The shiny bayonet plunged again and again. Once more, as had happened the night before, the room began to explode with color and motion.

In the background, as LaBianca rolled off the sofa onto the floor, I could hear his wife screaming from the bedroom: "What are you doing to my husband?" There were the sounds of some sort of scuffle and I ran in to join the girls. Mrs. LaBianca was in a corner of the room, still hooded with the pillowcase, swinging a large lamp (the wire was wrapped around her head) in an arc that kept the two girls from getting close to her. The bayonet had greater range and I struck out time after time, even after the woman had fallen to the floor.

Katie had run into the living room at some point and now she returned, saying, "He's still alive!"

I went back to the living room and used the bayonet again, over and over. Suddenly Charlie's face clicked in my head, as I heard the words he had sent me off with the night before: ". . . make it as gruesome as you can." Out of some horrible part of my brain an image formed and I reached down and carved WAR on the bare belly below me. Later-while I was washing away the LaBiancas' blood in their own shower—Katie would add to the grotesque picture by stabbing the dead man fourteen times (with an ivory-handled carving fork that she left wobbling in his stomach) and by planting a small steak knife in his neck, both these weapons coming from the LaBiancas' kitchen drawers.

After I'd finished my butchery on the man, I went back to the bedroom and told Leslie to help Katie stab the woman, even though it was obvious that Rosemary LaBianca was already dead. Leslie obeyed me, striking mainly on the exposed buttocks, but with none of the enthusiasm that Katie showed.

We started looking through the house, rifling drawers, opening closets—partly for money (we did find a bag of coins) and also for a change of clothes for me. While I washed off the bayonet in the bathroom sink and showered, the girls wrote on the walls and refrigerator door in blood: RISE, DEATH TO PIGS and Katie's misspelled HEALTER SKELTER. I changed into an old pair of brown khaki pants and a shirt of Mr. LaBianca's. We took some milk and cheese from the refrigerator. After making sure that the girls had wiped everything for fingerprints, I led them out the back door, patting the head of the dog that had followed us everywhere through the house as we left.

Charlie and the others were gone. I'd later learn that, while the three of us wandered through the Los Feliz district—getting lost and walking in circles for hours—

Charlie was planting Mrs. LaBianca's wallet in the rest room of a gas station in Sylmar (thinking it was a black neighborhood) and trying to set up the murder of a young actor Linda Kasabian knew in Venice, an attempt that Linda foiled by deliberately going to the wrong apartment door.

As we walked on in the predawn darkness, we came across a reservoir. I threw the bayonet out as far as I could into the water. Finally, half an hour later, we settled down under a tree in a vacant lot, waiting for dawn.

Once the sky started to lighten, we began walking again. I was still carrying my bloody clothes and when we found a large cardboard box full of trash at the curb, I pushed them down under the grass and garbage. Shortly afterward we met a man coming out for his morning paper and got directions to the Golden State Freeway.

We were picked up in a beat-up, multicolored car by a hippie who was also a night guard at Griffith Park. Ironically, he knew Spahn Ranch; he'd been there about a year before and thought he recognized the girls. While Leslie played up to him enough to get us a ride all the way to Chatsworth, we pretended we knew nothing about the ranch and were just on our way up to Big Sur. Apparently Leslie did her job on the guy too well, because after having breakfast with us (we spent most of the time telling him about Helter Skelter, never mentioning what we had just done to bring it down, and paid for the food out of the bag of coins we'd stolen from the LaBianca house), he kept insisting on taking us all the way to wherever we were going. Even after we finally got out of the car and took a long way around the back of the ranch to avoid letting him see us on the road, he turned up at Spahn later in the day, still looking for Leslie.

Charlie had already gone back into the hills to a camp we had by a waterfall, so I didn't see him. The girls disappeared and I flopped down on a mattress in one of the buildings, ready to sleep.

As I lay there, my mind raced and turned with images from the past two nights, like some horrible light show all full of red glare and frantic motion. Yet I felt nothing for what had been done to seven innocent people and an unborn child. Charlie had killed all that sort of feeling in me, just as I had killed those seven strangers.

I wondered what would happen this next night and the night after that. Although Susan Atkins's later claim that we had a death list of famous Hollywood stars was untrue, Charlie had made it clear that two nights would not be the end of it, that we would do more and more killing until either the blacks or the whites took matters into their own hands — and Helter Skelter would begin.

I have no doubt that things would have continued just as Charlie planned — for another night, for three more nights, ten, however long — if later that Sunday afternoon my mother had not called Willis Carson in Los

Angeles and asked him to get in touch with me because she hadn't had a word from her son in six months.

That call, and Willis's to the ranch that followed, set up my lie about the F.B.I. having come to my parents' home in Copeville, accusing me of murder. And that lie stopped the killing and sent us all to the desert where, nearly two months later, I refused to murder again for Manson and headed home to Copeville, with its peeling white wood and railroad, home to the store and the gas pumps and the kitchen-back to the world I thought I'd blasted out of my mind forever.

He's a Runner

My parents seemed like strangers to me, characters from a movie I'd seen once but nearly forgotten. Copeville was a cardboard town, a city in a dream. I was home, after so much, but home was nowhere. Charlie was my only home, my only reality, and I'd left him in the desert. Now, as unreal as everything around me seemed, so, too, did Manson and his Death Valley kingdom seem unreal. Everything was splintered, broken, disjointed. The only certainty was that unless Helter Skelter came down soon (And did I really think it would?), I would be caught. That thought did not particularly frighten or even concern me. I was too burned out to feel much of anything; it was simply a fact that sat quietly somewhere in the back of my blistered head.

My mother tried to take charge of things. She got me to the doctor, talked to me, worked to pick up the frayed ends of our family life. But it was obvious that something had happened to me, something that it would take more than good sense and home cooking to make right. I slept most of the time, ate little — and threw up, whenever I tried to please her by downing one of her huge Texas meals. I didn't wash, just lay around, watching television blindly with the shades drawn, screaming at my parents to shut up if they tried to speak to me.

Each day it seemed as though I got more confused. Added to all the turmoil that had been boiling in my mind even before I'd run away from Charlie, there was now the pull of home and family and habit, reminding me what I'd been and known. Was Charlie right? Were these people I'd called parents really pigs? Did this apparently stable world of familiar sights and sounds and smells tremble on the edge of extinction, waiting for its destruction? Or was everything my parents and their simple, honest lives represented the real truth? Did things make sense in a way I'd once thought they did? Or was it true, as Charlie said, that no sense is sense?

The once comfortable but now new and strange world of my family and my past loomed with greater intensity and reality, while the vivid, magical world that Charlie had given me faded daily until I could hardly hold on to it. It was as if my consciousness were being torn in half.

Finally I couldn't take it anymore. After about a week, I tricked my parents out of some money, got my father to drive me to Dallas to "see a friend," and then called them and announced that I was going back to Los Angeles to pick up the insurance money due me from the automobile accident in January of 1968.

I did not go to Los Angeles. I flew to Mexico and wandered aimlessly through the resort communities around Puerto Vallarta for a week or two, making friends among the young transients and scoring my first grass since the drugs had run out in the desert. But it was no good — Charlie was pulling me, and my fear was pushing me. I flew to Los Angeles and spent several days in a cheap hotel on the beach at Venice. As in Mexico, I seemed to be waiting for something to happen, but I didn't know what. I picked up some acid and hung around with other young people on the beach who were like me, with nothing else to do. Like me, but different; they didn't have my demons dancing through their heads at night. I decided to go to Hawaii and look up some people I'd known when I was with the Family. Maybe the Islands would be far enough away from everything to let me rest and forget.

I could only afford a one-way fare out of what was left of the money I'd taken from my parents, and shortly after I arrived in Hawaii a girl I brought back to my motel stole all that I had left beyond the price of the ticket. I ended up sleeping on the beach under a canoe. It was not as picturesque as it sounds—it rained a lot, the nights were cold, and even with the starvation diet I'd grown accustomed to in the desert, I still needed to eat occasionally. During the few days I was in Los Angeles I'd obtained a temporary driver's license under the name of Charles Smith, so I finally used the card as identification to get part-time work in a carpet-cleaning plant. What money I made at the job kept me going until I met a young Canadian on the beach one day, lifted the key to his motel room while he was sleeping, and stole enough money out of his room to buy a ticket back to L.A. Like Charlie said: *There is no right; there is no wrong.*

The first thing I did when I arrived in Los Angeles was buy a cheap cassette tape recorder and the tape of the Beatles' *Abbey Road* album. The four English rock stars had talked to me once before in their songs; maybe they'd have something to tell me now, some direction to give. I didn't really need any direction, though: I knew where I was going — back to Charlie.

I used the last of my money on bus fare to Trona, the gritty desert town I'd left only weeks before. Getting a large plastic jug of water, I started off on foot across the desert for Golar Wash, playing the Beatles' tape all the way. I walked for miles over the arid flatlands and then climbed a line of hills that lay between Trona and the valley below the Wash. I still had some of the acid I'd gotten in Venice and I dropped it periodically, pushing on through the wasteland. Charlie was my only goal.

It says something about my state of mind that after half a day and a night of walking, when I had just about reached the bottom of the Wash, I was suddenly certain that if I did go back to Charlie, he would kill me. It was sometime after midnight, but I turned back at once, ready to cross those hills and salt flats all over again to run away from the god I had, up to then, been so desperately seeking. On my way across the valley, I came upon the trailer of an old prospector whom we'd met several times while I was still with the Family. He, too, was called Tex and when I knocked on his door at two in the morning he told me that Charlie and all the others had been arrested. He wasn't sure why, but he thought it had something to do with car theft and arson. I'd better get out of the area, he said, and as quickly as possible.

The old man drove me down to Ridgecrest himself, about fifteen miles south of Trona. The next day, October 30, I once more called my folks and asked for money to fly home to them. This time they were more cautious, demanding that I promise to stay. I agreed and I kept my promise — until the time came when where I stayed or where I went was no longer something over which I had any control.

Back in Texas I tried again to settle into the life I'd known. I did odd jobs, helped my father add on to his store, fended off my mother's urging that I start looking for a serious job. I still was living in my own peculiar world, caught between Charlie and my past, lost in the cracks between two separate, incompatible realities. I occasionally consoled myself with the attentions of a girl I'd known during my college years. We'd smoke grass together and take rides and make love in the fashion I'd learned from the Family and that she would later describe in court and to the press as "animalistic."

My family — and it seemed strange to say that word without meaning Charlie and the others — made no secret of their concern for me. What had happened? What terrible thing in California had turned the son they'd been so proud of into this vacant-eyed, listless stranger who flew into rages without warning and spent hours lying in bed in his darkened room? On Thanksgiving all the relatives got together in my mother's living room and, sometime during the meal that I could barely touch, my sister's mother-in-law-knowing I'd been in California and anxious to find something that might make me join in the conversation — asked me casually, "Say, did they ever find out who killed that Sharon Tate and all those others?"

The moment seemed to last forever as I was torn between screaming, "You're looking at him!" and bolting. Finally I shook my head and tried to act interested in the food. I avoided her for the rest of the day.

On November 30, I took a drive with my rediscovered girl friend. We had a quiet day at a nearby lake, sitting on a blanket, talking. For some reason, I felt I could relax around her, and we even wove fantasy plans of running away to Northern California together. She was very bored with Texas, and California had the same allure for her it had once held — it seemed like an eternity ago — for me. It almost seemed possible that there might be a future.

When I got home that afternoon, my father and my mother's brother, Maurice Montgomery, were waiting for me. As soon as I walked into the dim, musty light of the store and saw the two of them together, my father's weathered face staring at me in pain and disbelief, I knew what had happened. The running was over.

I found out later that, shortly before I got back from the lake, Maurice had been visited by Deputy Sheriff Albert Bennet from McKinney, who told him that I was wanted for murder in California. A call had just come through from the Los Angeles County District Attorney's office. My uncle and the deputy had then walked over to the store to talk to my father. A few minutes before I got home the deputy had headed back to McKinney.

Now my father and uncle faced me. My father had always been a direct man: "Charles," he said, "do you know anything about a murder in California?" My answer was equally direct: "No."

When I walked into the kitchen a few moments later, my mother looked up with one of her smiles. "You know what," I told her with all the confused innocence I could muster, ". . . they're trying to get me for some kind of murder in California."

She had already taken a lot and she would have to take much more. As I crossed toward my bedroom she called after me, "It can't be so! Charles, do you . . . did you have a fight, maybe . . . and the boy could have died after you left or something?"

I looked her in the eye: "I didn't kill anybody." She told me to put on my best clothes for the ride into McKinney. I went into the bathroom and flushed down the toilet the last few tabs of the acid I'd bought in Venice.

As the three of us rode the twenty-five miles into McKinney — my father, Uncle Maurice, and me — I never spoke. The thought of escape crossed my mind, but I felt too weak to do anything but lean back and stare out the window at the familiar flat landscape whipping by. It was all out of my hands now. I was almost relieved.

When we got to the sheriff's office in the big stone jail — just off the main square where the Collin County Courthouse punctuates the low-slung town — my second cousin, County Sheriff Tom Montgomery, called California again for more information but was told nothing except that I was to be held until Los Angeles detectives got to McKinney and that I was dangerous. As he led me to a cell with an embarrassed, apologetic grin, my cousin Tom said, "I think we'll be able to clear all this up quick enough. We know for sure you didn't commit no murder." I walked into the cell without answering him.

By late the next day, the story had hit the wire services, reporters had started calling my parents at home, and photographers and news people were descending on McKinney in droves. My parents had to fight their way through a large crowd to get into the jail.

It was front-page news. Los Angeles Police Chief Edward Davis gave a press conference to announce that warrants had been issued for the arrest of Patricia Krenwinkel, Linda Kasabian, and Charles Watson (Charlie, Susan and Leslie would be named later) for the murders of Sharon Tate, Jay Sebring, Abigail Folger, Voytek Frykowski, Steven Parent, Rosemary LaBianca and Leno LaBianca. He told the two hundred reporters from around the world that the crime of the decade had been solved.

A few days later my father painted over the WATSON on the front of the store he'd taken half a lifetime to build.

Inside

It would seem a simple matter — once a warrant has been issued on seven counts of murder — to extradite the accused for trial. Los Angeles Deputy District Attorney Vincent Bugliosi certainly thought it would be. In fact, I ended up remaining in Texas for nine months before I was taken to California. My extradition case went all the way to the United States Supreme Court (which, in declining to admit it, effectively sent me to Los Angeles) and the major result of the nine-month delay was to grant me a separate trial from Charlie and the women.

My attorney in Texas was Bill Boyd, the son of Roland Boyd (who'd counseled me and my family several years before in the matter of the stolen typewriters). At that time the younger Boyd had been district attorney for Collin County, but now — his term completed — he had returned to private practice in the family firm. Roland Boyd was a big man with the courtly manner and grand Southern sheen of another generation of gentlemen, but Bill was a mild, soft-spoken man with glasses, the beginnings of baldness, and a conservative taste in his clothes. He was also, as the next nine months would prove, a tenacious fighter for what he believed was right.

We had our first meeting the morning after my arrest, in a dingy little upstairs room at the jail, a room which would become very familiar to me over the next nine months. My parents were present, and I continued to insist that I had no idea what the warrant was all about. (Chief Davis had not yet held his press conference-it took place at 2:00 P.M. Los Angeles time.) It was only after they had gone back to Copeville that I called Boyd back and told him that there was one thing that had happened in California—I had been involved in the Tate LaBianca killings. Lawyers, like poker players, need poise—and Bill Boyd handled the moment well. We would need to talk a lot, he said.

Two detectives from Los Angeles arrived later that day, assuring the waiting newsmen that they would be taking me back to Los Angeles within a few days at the most (apparently assuming I would waive extradition). They had not reckoned with Bill Boyd.

At the time of my arrest, there was only one piece of "hard" evidence (physical evidence as opposed to the testimony of witnesses) against me: a fingerprint taken from the front door of the Tate house which matched a fingerprint of mine made when I was arrested on my belladonna trip of April 23. (Since the maid at the Tate residence had washed down the door the day of the murders, there was no way this print could have been explained away as the result of an earlier visit, even if I'd wanted to try.)

The D.A.'s office knew a great deal more than what that one print could have told them, however. They'd gotten information from some of the girls arrested in the mid-October raid on Barker Ranch and also from Straight Satan Danny DeCarlo and a buddy of his — Al Springer — who'd spent the two days after the murders at Spahn. Most of all, Sadie hadn't been able to resist the urge to share her secret. She'd done a lot of talking to some of her fellow prisoners at the Sybil Brand Institute for Women in Los Angeles.

Sadie had been arrested with the rest of the Family during the three-day raid on Barker Ranch, and while she was still in custody in Independence, Kitty Lutesinger (Bobby Beausoleil's girlfriend who was five months pregnant with his child) had implicated her in the Hinman murder. When interviewed by detectives on that case, Sadie had talked freely, throwing all the blame on Bobby. She apparently thought the police already knew everything she had to say, anyway.

She was booked for murder and transferred to Los Angeles and Sybil Brand. While she was there, she began trying to impress some of the other inmates — first Virginia Graham, then later Ronnie Howard — with tales of the Family and Charlie, finally confiding that she had been one of the Tate-LaBianca killers. (In fact, she had never been inside the LaBianca house, a point she finally made clear to Ronnie Howard. She exaggerated other things, however, such as claiming that she had stabbed Sharon and then tasted her blood.) After a great deal of trouble with prison bureaucracy, Ronnie

Howard finally managed to reach the D.A. with what she had heard.

Later, Susan-Sadie herself told her story to the D.A.'s office and then to the grand jury (a more factual version that left out her claim to having stabbed Sharon Tate) and even had it published in the Los Angeles Times and various European papers as "Susan Atkins' Story of Two Nights of Murder." However, by the time she and the others were tried, Susan would have repudiated her confession and the printed account. During the trial itself—along with Katie and Leslie — she would try to lay the entire blame for the murders on me, thus absolving Charlie. By that time, though, the true story had been told by Linda Kasabian, the gentle, frightened girl who never actually harmed anyone (and, in fact, saved one life-the actor in Venice) and begged us to stop what was happening at Cielo Drive after it was too late. Linda received immunity for her testimony, though she didn't request it, and later explained that she did not run directly to the police when the slaughter began at Cielo Drive because she was afraid of what Manson might do to her little girl, Tanya, who had been left at Spahn Ranch. She did escape with Tanya several days after the LaBianca murders.

Much of this was months down the road, however. At the time of my arrest, the Los Angeles County District Attorney's office had a fingerprint, Susan's story (as told to Ronnie Howard), and testimony from a number of Family members and fringe followers like Danny DeCarlo. They also had a mountain of publicity.

It was the publicity that led Bill Boyd to fight my extradition for nine months. As Boyd explained it to me, pretrial publicity is a peculiar thing. Traditionally, a juror could not be disqualified (beyond a certain number of automatic challenges granted both prosecution and defense) for simply being exposed to it. Rather, only if that publicity had prejudiced the prospective juror's opinion as to the guilt or innocence of the accused was the person not permitted to sit in judgment.

Considering our modern means of mass communication, this made sense. Otherwise, no one but recluses and the simple could serve on juries for widely publicized, "high profile" crimes. However, the question of whether or not a juror's opinions had been influenced by what he or she had seen, heard, or read before a trial was pretty much up to that person to decide. If a prospective juror claimed not to be prejudiced, most courts would accept that claim at face value.

Such was the traditional interpretation of the law. But there were precedents for Boyd's contention that if pretrial publicity is extensive enough, no one exposed to that barrage of prejudicial information can reasonably be expected to form an unbiased opinion strictly on the merits of the case as presented in court. An important decision was *Rideau v. the State of Louisiana*, in which the United States Supreme Court had ruled that — after a confession made by the accused was videotaped by the police and shown three times on local television — none of the 29,000 people in the area from which the jury was drawn was qualified. Thus, the High Court reversed the conviction and ordered a new trial.

That was the precedent. What was unprecedented was Boyd's contention that the massive publicity of the Tate-LaBianca case, combined with the sensational nature of the crimes themselves, made the entire state of California incapable of providing me with a fair trial and that the venue should therefore be changed to a court outside that state. To protect my right to an unbiased jury, he argued, I should not be returned to the state of California. The fact that California had no legal provision for transferring a criminal case to a jurisdiction outside of the state was their problem, not ours, he said. The right of the accused to an unprejudiced jury superseded whatever difficulties that right might raise for prosecutors or courts.

Boyd was no cynic. He knew I was guilty and his intent was not to get me off. He simply believed firmly that under our system of justice every person-no matter how obvious his guilt or how horrible his crime-deserves a fair trial. He also believed, given what he was learning from me about the Family and Charlie's control and use of consciousness-altering drugs, that a fair judgment of my guilt would involve an argument of "diminished capacity," since he was convinced I had reached a condition under Manson's domination where I was not in control of, nor fully responsible for, my actions. He was certain that these considerations would be lost on a jury in California, especially Southern California, where not only had there been tremendous publicity and widespread fear generated by the killings, but where a local judge would be under greater pressure from his constituency to "hang" the accused, whatever the circumstances.

Whether or not his concerns were justified, Bill Boyd insisted up to the time I was finally extradited on September 11 of the following year that sending me to California would not serve justice. While I spent month after month in the little cell in the Collin County Jail, all I knew was that the longer he kept me in Texas, the longer it would be before I had to face whatever was coming.

While later published accounts of my "special treatment" while I was in jail in McKinney were exaggerated, it was not a terrible life. The cell was very small and stuffy, with the noise and greasy steam of the nearby kitchen pouring in most of the day. But my parents had brought me a small television and Boyd provided me with a tape deck and some Beatles' tapes. I did yoga exercises which Charlie had taught us at Spahn and back bends and sometimes I ran in place.

I was still a vegetarian, so my mother brought me food each time my folks visited (once a day until sometime into the next year, when they started coming every other day). Since there was no attorney/client conference room in the old jail in McKinney, whenever they or Boyd came to see me, we'd all troop upstairs to the dingy office on the second floor. There was an adjacent bathroom with a tub, so I'd bathe and talk to them through the door.

Boyd claims that my cousin Tom never stretched the law on my behalf, that he simply enforced it more rigidly for my protection than was usually the case. Many extraditions, Boyd said, were little more than kidnappings arranged with the connivance of local law enforcement, since-once the suspect is in the state requesting extradition — questions as to how he got there become moot. Boyd explained that Tom was within his rights in refusing to let the Los Angeles detectives even see me. But I must confess that, as the months wore on, I was often sent upstairs to meet my folks or my lawyer without any guard or restraints. I would walk by the open door to the sidewalk outside without anything but my own laziness to keep me from skipping. To be fair, in the eyes of my jailers I was a model prisoner who earned their respect and confidence. And I think in all their minds was the conviction that "those people" out in California had to be mistaken, that a good hometown boy like me couldn't have done what "they" were claiming. Sometimes I'd fantasize bolting out that open door and starting to run — down the dusty streets, out into the level countryside where there was plenty of space and air — maybe going fishing. Each time, though, I'd glance out at the light and life and then turn and trudge upstairs.

I don't remember when I finally told my parents the truth. Whenever it was, they refused to believe me, at least my mother did. She would sob, insisting I wasn't guilty, that the drugs were just twisting my mind, and I'd torment her by going on and on about how beautiful Sharon's face had been as she was pleading for her life, just before I cut her. Sometimes I thought my head would split open with the effort of trying to convince them that it was all true. Sometimes I'd explode with rage, attacking my mother verbally, telling her if she didn't act better I'd tell the deputies not to let her come and see me anymore. Out of the hell that was stewing inside me, I caused those two helpless people more pain than they had probably ever imagined was possible. But I couldn't see that at the time. All I knew was the warfare going on inside my brain between Charlie's reality and theirs, two great spiritual powers battling for my soul.

My other Family didn't forget me. I got letters from the girls who weren't in jail, especially Squeaky Fromme and Gypsy (Catherine Share). "Why haven't you written?" they kept asking (Boyd had told me to sever all contact with the Family), and in one note Squeaky advised me to get in contact with Daye Shinn, a lawyer in Los Angeles who was representing Susan Atkins and seemed willing to go along with the Family's plan to protect Charlie at all costs. "If you contact any other lawyer it will be more difficult for us to help you," one letter advised. But mostly it was just rambling, rhyming nonsense:

". . . circle as in circle as in living o'bla . . . fool baby drool spool of thread in my bed, as in yours as is all our love . . . ." (In this and the following quote, punctuation and spelling are as in the original.) Sometimes it wasn't hard to read the message behind the string of words, as when one of them wrote:

> *Time to call time from behind you the illusion has been just a dream. Valley of death and I'll find you now is when on a sunshine beam songs from up out of the dungeons from between the teeth of the lions who know not what they do — & do not wish to. Here we belong in love — the song always sung — the voices in separate cells the heart together as One dwells in toes and fingers and soft dreams and the holecost [sic] to come quick upon their heads. If they could be warned — but they can't for they live in the past and know nothing of now.*

No sense is sense, and beneath the strange flow the sense was all too clear. Don't give up. Helter Skelter may be taking its time, but it will come and we are one—one with each other, one with Charlie, one in waiting. But were we? Was I? Was I part of Charlie's Family or my parents' family—their life or his? Who was I? What was I? Was there an I?

Jailhouse Religion

As I waited in my little graffiti-covered cell in the Collin County Jail, I started hearing about that pale-faced Jesus of my childhood again. I refused to see any ministers, but my parents let me know they were praying for me. My mother even suggested I might want my old Bible. I was more interested in the magazines they brought — they were good for something. I could cut brightly colored pictures out of them and paste together surreal visions of the Beatles' "Yellow Submarine" characters popping out of flowers and huge insects and animals gliding across purple landscapes in a scrapbook I was making. Sometimes at night those visions would leap from the pages into my head, mingling with blood and Charlie and the desert and knives, and then the other prisoners would call for the guards because I was going crazy in my cell, throwing myself against the bars and screaming.

The flashbacks didn't come very often, though. Mostly it was just passing time, doing nothing. Outside, Bill Boyd fought the extradition step by step, using every device our legal system offered him to keep me in Texas.

In his book *Helter Skelter*, Los Angeles Prosecutor Vincent Bugliosi, understandably frustrated by his inability to get me out to California for trial with the others, states that Roland Boyd was campaign manager in a race for state attorney general by the very judge (David Brown) who granted "delay after delay after delay" in the extradition request. The implication that the Boyds used political influence to stretch the law is simply not true: Roland Boyd was, in fact, not campaign manager for anybody running for any state office; Judge Brown issued only one thirty-day continuance; and the law was not stretched. The normal processes of appeal, if followed to the end, naturally take nearly a year. It was just that no one had ever fought an extradition case as thoroughly as Bill Boyd did mine.

Early in December, a few days after my twenty-fourth birthday — the first I would spend in jail — two lawyers from Los Angeles arrived in McKinney, announcing that they were my attorneys. These men had represented my claim in the accident case several years before, and we'd smoked grass together a few times, but beyond that, the only thing that could possibly have brought the two of them to Texas was the smell of publicity and money. They insisted to the news-hungry press people who were stuck in this very small, very boring town that I was being held incommunicado and that they were being kept from their client by the unscrupulous Mr. Boyd. It finally ended up in the courthouse down the street from the jail. I was asked by Judge David Brown if I wanted to talk to them or be represented by them, and as I stared up at the stained ceiling of the old courthouse that looked more like a Baptist church than a court of law I murmured, "No . . . ."

Since Boyd was planning to argue against extradition on the basis of pretrial publicity, he had me wear a coat over my head for the short walk from the elevators to the courtroom (I'd been brought in a panel truck from the jail to the courthouse basement). We were not going to provide any publicity of our own, he said. Eventually Judge Brown ruled that each of the frustrated cameramen could take a limited number of pictures in the courtroom while we were in recess.

On December 14, the *Los Angeles Times* exploded with Sadie's front-page account of **TWO NIGHTS OF MURDER**, and Boyd had more support for his case. He had hired Bill Reed, formerly of the local McKinney paper and now on the staff of the *Dallas Times-Herald*, to do a complete survey of all news coverage of the Tate-La Bianca cases in California and Reed ended up with 114 exhibit samples. In printed material alone it ran the gamut from *Ladies' Home Journal* to a sleazy *Pageant* article that tried to link the evils of Hollywood "sex clubs" to the deaths. This impressive display of the saturation coverage in the state (it nearly equaled that of the Kennedy assassination) did not convince the Texas secretary of state. He granted the extradition on January 5, 1970, and the next day the order was signed by the governor. Boyd immediately filed a writ of *habeas corpus* in Judge Brown's court and on the sixteenth the judge granted a thirty-day continuance. But on February 16 he ruled that, while there had indeed been extensive press coverage, there was no evidence of irresponsibility by the media (". . . sensational events cannot be accurately presented in prosaic terms . . . ") and that any decision about detrimental pretrial publicity should be made by a California court, not his own.

The process of appeals began — the Court of Criminal Appeals of Texas, the United States District Court for the Eastern District of Texas, the United States Supreme Court. Each was denied, but with each new appeal, two more months were allowed by law for preparation and presentation of briefs, plus the time required for the judge or judges involved to reach a decision. Finally the Supreme Court declined to admit the case for hearing — and it was over. I was on my way to California. The trial of Charlie, Sadie, Katie, and Leslie was already in its third month.

I left for Los Angeles on September 11, 1970, over a year after the murders. Bill Boyd's last words to me were: "Don't say anything to anyone. You have the right to remain silent." And all the way to California, as newsmen with video machines and cameras tried to get at me and the two detectives who were with me tried to interrogate me, I wouldn't open my mouth, even to the stewardess. During processing at the "Glass House" in downtown Los Angeles, I refused to answer even the simplest question. Boyd had said not to talk, so I would not talk. This barrier of silence would eventually drive me deeper and deeper into myself, working on me, building with so much else inside my head that it seemed as if I would lose not only my sanity but my life itself.

Late on the night of my arrival, as I sat in my cell high up in that enormous Los Angeles City jail, the earth began to tremble. Charlie had always said there'd be an earthquake soon, just before Helter Skelter. It would be one of the signs, he said.

The next day I was transferred from the city jail to the sprawling county installation just northeast of the Civic Center. I still kept my silence and it was strange — the longer you went without speaking, the easier the muteness became. Words no longer flew to your mouth; it was as if the connection between mind and tongue slowly withered. I did finally talk to the chaplain there, John Goffigan, although at first I was certain even this quiet, gentle man was a spy for the D.A. My mother had written him and sent a Bible that he gave me along with several other books. Back in McKinney I hadn't been interested in reading any Bible, but things had been different then. I'd grown accustomed to my little cell in the Collin County Jail. I'd had my family nearby. It had been a world I understood, for all the twisting and turning that went on inside my head. Now suddenly I was part of a huge institution where everywhere I looked there were staring eyes and hostility, from guards and inmates alike. I was immediately the object of morbid curiosity and violent hatred. Here was the creep who'd butchered Sharon Tate when she was eight months pregnant!

I don't blame anyone for what he felt, and I know I didn't make things any easier when I refused to talk to the few men who did stop at my cell bars and try to make conversation. I was a stranger in a strange land, unconnected and apart, an object to be stared at by a hostile world. I was cut off from my family and the Family that had replaced it, cut off from both realities I'd lived, cut off even from the one outsider I'd been able to trust since my arrest, Bill Boyd. In a world like that, the only place to go is in. But *in* for me was a confused country. Sometimes I felt like my own mother's son again; at other moments I was still and always Charlie's child.

Partly to get relief from everything that wouldn't stop churning through my head, partly to find something to focus on besides the negative vibrations coming at me from every direction, I started reading the Bible my mother had sent — sometimes the Psalms, sometimes verses I'd memorized long ago as a child in the Copeville Methodist Church. Often I'd just open the black book at random. I understood very little of what I read, but that didn't seem to matter. The words washed over me like soothing water; they made me feel at peace. They were the place of stillness in my world of constant light and noise.

The God of my childhood had been that hazy blond man with long hair and insipid features who smiled out of Bible illustrations and Sunday-school calendars. He was often pictured nailed to a cross, with purple skies seething behind Him, though how He ended up there I was never sure. All I knew was that on Easter there was a lot of special music, flowers that made the church look like a funeral, and you wore new clothes and had ham for dinner. Perhaps that's exaggeration, but whatever I may have been able to rattle off in a Sunday-school class or evening devotional, I never really understood, or even bothered to wonder about the meaning of this Jesus whom I supposedly belonged to through personal experience (Of what?) and water baptism. That weak Messiah — behind whom stood a carping Judge with the face of an old man and the moral sensibilities of my mother—had never been more than some sort of touchstone for my assorted guilts. As I grew up, God rapidly became the least important thing in my all-American world.

The next god that came into my life was Charles Manson. His love was evident; I lived it. His Family gave me what seemed to be a new life, even as it took away all of mine, and he had his own peculiar baptism — drugs and fear and sex and death. But now it was beginning to look as if he, too, had failed me — or was it that I had failed him?

My mother's Jesus, the Stranger in the white robe or Manson, my Jesus, a stranger who became the self with a thousand faces and whose last face was death? And now, as I read the Bible which Chaplain Goffigan had given me, there was another Jesus, the real God. The events through which They revealed themselves were the familiar stories I'd heard as a child, but as I read now, the stories became something more than fairy tales about men in bathrobes. It was nothing I could put words to, hardly even a feeling, far less than belief . . . . Perhaps the name for it was hope.

While I had still been in Texas, Bill Boyd had made contact with a lawyer in California who'd agreed to take my case for $15,000. Somehow my family agreed to what was an astronomical figure for working people in Copeville, but when I got to Los Angeles and called the man, the figure had been raised considerably. During a visit to the jail the next day, the attorney kept talking about more and more money until finally, having passed $100,000, he told me he would need "unlimited funds" for my defense. I never saw him again until I was taken to court for arraignment. At that time he informed the judge that I could not afford counsel, and Sam Bubrick was appointed to handle my case, later to be joined by Maxwell Keith, Leslie Van Houten's attorney.

Sam Bubrick was a somewhat nervous, overweight man in his late fifties who seemed — at somewhere about five-foot-nine — a little short to me (I'm six-foot-two). He liked wide, flashy ties and would tear at his fingernails when he was under pressure. Keith was a few years younger and dressed more like the image of a lawyer I'd come to expect from Boyd — pinstriped suits and school ties. Somehow I always picture him as coughing — he was a chain-smoker. My first conversation with Bubrick was through a plate of glass, with the two of us talking into telephones in the visiting room at the Los Angeles County Jail. I was afraid to say much of anything to him. He wasn't Bill Boyd, so I had no reason to trust him, and besides, I was sure the conversation was being monitored.

The sense of being watched, trapped, observed, and overheard at every moment, awake or asleep, became the dominant reality of my existence. Each day the shell that held together what little was left of myself closed tighter and tighter. My physical body seemed to suck in on itself, drawing my arms and legs back into my belly. My body was shrinking slowly to a tiny dot of presence that one false wind could blow away forever. Yet the smaller my self got, the farther apart the pieces would float. I began to imagine that there were television cameras following me everywhere I went in the jail, hidden in dim corners and angles of walls. I was sure there were bugs in my cell and that every person except the chaplain who showed any interest in me was a spy sent by the police or the D.A. When Sam Bubrick would visit me, I'd tell him frantically that they were putting drugs in my food and that at night my hands glowed in the dark.

The confusion wouldn't stop, it would only pound at me, harder and harder, like some gigantic engine. Family member Bruce Davis was being held on the tier above me and, whenever he thought the guards couldn't hear, he'd call down messages to me from Charlie, which the girls who were free brought him in the visiting room. Day and night his voice would boom out in the metallic hollowness of the jail: "Cease to exist . . . remain one . . . Helter Skelter is coming down soon . . . ." Even the food became an enemy. They mixed together the meat and vegetables on the paper plate they shoved into the cell, so there was no way I could avoid eating flesh except by not eating at all.

I went on reading, even when I didn't understand what the black book was saying. Hour after hour I'd turn the pages of the Bible and let the words roll across the jagged edges of my mind. As I did, something else began to happen inside me, something that was perhaps the final straw to my sanity: I began tasting the reality of what I had actually done during those two nights of blood. It was no more than the tiniest spark of human feeling, somewhere deep inside my gut, but it was enough to drive me wild. Suddenly they were not nameless, impersonal things, not pigs — they were terrified men and women who had begged to be allowed to live, and I had battered and stabbed and shot the life out of them without mercy. It wasn't even so much guilt that racked me; it was the beginning of compassion. I began to throw myself against the bars, shaking them and screaming. I'd already let my cell become a smelly mess, my body steaming in its own filth. Now I started squeezing my toothpaste out onto the walkway through the bars and spattering the walls with food. I was taken to the hospital ward upstairs and put in restraints. Later, prosecution psychiatrists would claim I had faked much of my disintegration, but it was not true. All the little pieces just finally came unglued.

I seemed to improve a little in the hospital, so after a while I was sent back to my cell. It began all over again: Bruce's voice screaming down at me about hacksaws and escape and Helter Skelter, and the negative vibrations all around me driving me deeper and deeper into nothing.

When my weight dropped to 110 pounds from my usual 165 I was sent back upstairs. Once more I was bound to the cot with four-point restraints — both ankles and wrists — and now orderlies came and jabbed a tube down my nose. As humanitarian as forced feeding may sound, it is hell to live through. The sensitive membranes of the nose and throat are torn by the tubing and most of the sickening liquid being pumped into you is vomited back up, mingled with blood. Strapped on your back, it is all you can do to keep from drowning in it.

By this point I couldn't talk even if I wanted to — and Sam Bubrick was afraid I would die. He asked for three court psychiatrists to examine me, and they determined that I was regressing into a fetal state that could be terminal. I was insane, they said, totally incapable of standing trial. On October 29, Judge George Dell who had earlier ruled on Leslie's sanity — had me committed to Atascadero State Hospital for ninety-day observation.

"Jailhouse religion" they call it in cynical prison slang: the sudden desperate piety of an inmate who's up against it and hopes that God will somehow bail him out, a kind of bribe for an Almighty who has, up to that point, been of little interest to the new convert. Of course it often fades once the crisis has passed and it is often based on nothing but an overwhelming need to get out of trouble, with no thought for what God might ask of us. Of course. But despite all that, it was Jesus of Nazareth who said, "Come to Me, all of you that are carrying burdens more than you can bear . . . . I won't turn you away." (See Matthew 11:28; John 6:37.) I believe He hears. In fact, I know it. He heard me.

As I lay strapped on my back in the hospital, the words of the Twenty-third Psalm — one I'd memorized as a child and read again in the Bible my mother had sent — began to run through my head: "The Lord is my shepherd; I shall not want . . . ." I repeated the whole Psalm, over and over, with a sudden clarity of memory. First it was a prayer; then it became the answer to the prayer. I was suddenly aware of another presence in the stark hospital cell, not exactly visible, but unmistakably, powerfully there. It was this new Christ I'd been reading about. There was no doubt of it; this Son of God was saying: "Come to Me . . ." and He was there. As the Psalm continued to flow through my mind it was as if He took me to Himself, held me, and filled me with a peace and a quiet that left me sure that everything was going to be all right, no matter what came next. Whether I lived or died, I had nothing to fear: "Yea, though I walk through the valley of the shadow of death, I will fear no evil, for thou art with me." He was with me; I knew it and I could rest. It didn't matter anymore what happened — He would not desert me.

When I had been with Charlie, I'd stopped caring if I lived or died because I was dead already. Now it no longer mattered to me whether my physical life continued — because, alive or dead, I knew that Life Himself had made me alive in Him.

On Trial

I was held in Atascadero State Hospital from October 31, 1970, to February 14, 1971. The ambulance that took me up from the county jail passed fields of pumpkins, and I thought of Halloweens at home when I was a kid. Late that night, as we pulled off the freeway in Atascadero, I remembered the speeding ticket Dean Moorehouse and I had gotten two and a half years before in Terry Melcher's XKE. How had all that talk of love brought me to this?

I was too weak to walk, so was taken inside on a gurney. There were only two things in my mind: the certainty that Christ, whatever and whoever He was, was with me, so everything would be all right, and a warning from Sam Bubrick not to speak to anybody about the murders.

When I woke up the next morning, strapped to a cot, there was something strange happening: daylight was pouring into the room. At both Los Angeles jails you never saw real sunlight, only the glaring electric bulbs that ran night and day.

When I got a little stronger (they were spoon-feeding me), I was moved to a new room that had nothing but a mattress on the floor and a hole in one corner for a toilet. It was to be my home for three weeks, while the doctors and medical assistants spent hours talking with me, or rather at me. I responded very little, especially when they would probe for information about the killings. Finally, one afternoon I blurted out to one of the doctors, my chief tormentor, that Charlie had me so programmed that I could kill anyone, on any day, even him. I meant, if Charlie told me to, but the doctor screamed to the MTAs (Medical Trained Assistants who served as combination orderlies and guards): "He just threatened to kill me; you heard him!"

At night I was stripped to shorts and socks and given one thin blanket in the apparently unheated room. Even in California, winter nights are cold, and my strongest memory of the place is shivering in the dark. Later, a guard would tell me that this room was the last place the state of California had to put you—after that there was nothing left but a box.

I was eventually moved to a regular cell, and each day the main activity was trying to get me to eat and checking my weight to see when I would be strong enough to return to Los Angeles. Some of the MTAs (who assisted at so-called group therapy where we would sit in a circle of eight and try to think of things to say that would please them) were certain that I wasn't eating meat because I wanted to stay too sick to go to trial. One afternoon they took me into an empty office and held a piece of beef under my nose.

"Eat this," one of them told me.

"No."

I suddenly doubled over as another one of them started karate-chopping me on the neck and ribs. Then he popped me just under the sternum, and the next thing I knew I was waking up in an oxygen mask, my face and limbs blue. When I was conscious again, the three of them took me back to my room and stripped me, checking for bruises. Later, a hospital psychiatrist would pass this off in court as "wrestling therapy" intended to bring out my aggressions so I could "deal with them." This peculiar therapy was not all that unusual in Ward 14. Patients who got out of hand, or sometimes were simply disliked by certain MTAs, often disappeared into one of the back rooms for a therapeutic beating.

I finally got a job setting up the "chow carts" and was allowed extra vegetables as a reward. By February my weight was back up to 128 pounds, so I was sent to Los Angeles on a bus with a number of other inmates. It was like a vacation, sitting at the window and watching the countryside slide by, full of light and air and life. Even the freeway made me want to laugh for joy.

I'd only been back in the County Jail for a few days when I was called down to the visiting room. It was Brenda (Nancy Pitman) and one of the young boys who'd hung around on the edges of the Family. All I could do was stare at their foreheads — they had torn ragged 'X' marks in the flesh. Later I was told that they were copying Charlie, who did it to show the court that he had

'X-ed himself out of the establishment's world.' I refused to see any Family members again.

On March 29, 1971, Charlie, Susan, Leslie, and Katie were all found guilty of first-degree murder with a penalty of death. Susan turned to the jury and screamed: "Better lock your doors and watch your own kids." On April 19, Judge Charles Older formally sentenced each of them to the gas chamber. When the decision was announced, one of the Family girls who'd been keeping vigil outside the courthouse shrieked into waiting television cameras: "Death? That's what you're all going to get!"

On May 10 I entered a plea of "not guilty by reason of insanity" before Judge Adolph Alexander, who by coincidence was a personal friend of Sam Bubrick's.

I spent the following summer talking to psychiatrist after psychiatrist, having electroencephalograms made, taking tests, telling Bubrick everything I could remember about my use of drugs, Manson's domination, and my mental state at the time of the murders. Bubrick was convinced we could at least have the charge reduced from first- to second-degree murder on the basis of diminished mental capacity, if not win an acquittal and have me hospitalized.

When I was alone, I'd read the Bible. Gradually, more of it began to open up to me. Things I should have known all my life — raised in a religious home and taken to a Christian church — somehow now started to make sense to me for the first time. My understanding was groping and incomplete, but I caught the first glimpses of what I would know more clearly later: that my own horrors were part of a larger horror, a whole world gone wrong because creatures made by and for a loving God (not the bearded judge I'd imagined when I was a kid) tried to be gods themselves and run their world without Him. That in no way took away my responsibility for what I'd done, what I'd allowed myself to become, but it explained why, when I had opened myself to whatever was around me in this broken world, what flooded the emptiness inside me was demonic and deadly.

I began to see, too, that even for guilt as gross as mine, a penalty had already been paid. A death penalty, carried by God Himself in His Son Jesus. I could see easily how the power of death and destruction ruled this present world, or seemed to — I'd served that power, expressed through one diabolical man who wanted to be a god. Slowly I began to see, as well, the power of God's love to overcome that death and destruction, to heal it, not just abstractly but immediately and specifically — for me. Even for me.

If my self had been shattered into a thousand disjointed pieces, the God who made that self to begin with could mend it. If I had so torn apart my consciousness by a dozen different mind-bending drugs that I was barely human anymore, God could heal what I'd done to myself.

But what about what I'd done to others, to seven others and one never born? Nothing could make that right. No, Chaplain Goffigan told me, but it could be forgiven.

Somehow, in all those years in church, I'd missed the incredible news that church was supposed to be all about: that the Creator of all there is had become part of His own Creation; that He did it for love and that He let His creatures, people like us, kill Him so that we could live — so that we could be free from the death that was the only thing left for us once we turned away from Life Himself. That was what love was all about: God, dying for us in His Son, to put an end to the death that is our living without Him and to make new life out of the death that seems to end our lives.

Charlie's trip had been death, but this Jesus promised life. Charlie had taught me to fear so I could love, but this Bible said in 1 John 4:18 that perfect love destroyed all our fear. If only it could be true. Yet it was! Hadn't I learned that when I was strapped to the cot in the hospital and He'd made it so clear that He was with me? That was what love was like, what I'd felt then.

Slowly — as I read and tried haltingly to talk to God with words in my head — the cross I'd seen in all those old Bible illustrations made more and more sense, because at that cross the Son of God had taken everything that mankind had bent and twisted and perverted in God's good Creation onto Himself.

If it was true, that meant that God didn't turn away from anything I'd dragged myself into. God didn't turn away from Family members squirming together in mindless sexual orgies — He took that on Himself and nailed it to the cross. God didn't turn away from the destruction I'd wreaked on my mind and body — that too was spiked through and crucified. He didn't even turn away from those two nights of butchery. He took all that anguish and horror. He took the guilt of my bloody hands, and that, too — even that, if I would let go of it — could be nailed up, done away with. It seemed impossible, too good to be true, but the Bible said it and Chaplain Goffigan said it. Something inside of me said it, too. There could be light, even in my darkness.

I might have to die for what I'd done, as Charlie and Sadie and Leslie and Katie were supposed to die, but even if I were executed, the eternal death, the death of the true Bottomless Pit that Charlie so appropriately distorted into his hellish vision of heaven, that death was broken by Christ for me. All I had to do was accept what had been done for me — say yes.

As best as I could in my mental state, I think I did say yes, I think the yes had somehow been said several months before as I lay strapped to that cot repeating Psalm 23 over and over. But it was a yes that would take time to have its effect.

During my trial, Prosecutor Bugliosi would insist that my claim to feel remorse was untrue, just as my apparent mental collapse was a fake as far as he was concerned.

But he was wrong. As much as my scarred conscience was capable of feeling anything at the time, I had genuine sorrow for what I had done, for the unspeakable pain I had caused both the victims and those who loved them. But he was right if he meant that what I felt was still far less than what a person who had not spent two years blasting all trace of humanity out of him would feel. When I came to trial on August 2, 1971, I was more than I had been when Manson had reduced me to nothing, but I was a long way from what God, by His grace, would make me, and farther still from what I trust I'll someday be in Him.

It was strange, but sitting in Judge Alexander's courtroom, listening to the trial that would presumably determine whether I lived or died, I felt practically nothing. Even the fact that my mother was in the audience each day, seeing and hearing all the horror of what the son she'd been so proud of had done and become, even that didn't really touch me. When she came up to, the defense table one morning early in the trial and put her arms around me, I pulled away. I didn't want to feel any more than I had to, there was enough reason for anguish already.

The first witnesses were Paul Tate, Sharon's father, and Steven Parent's dad, Wilfred. Watching them, listening to them give evidence as to when and where they'd last seen the people they'd loved so much, the people I'd destroyed, I felt more deeply than ever before the reality of what we'd done those nights, but I couldn't show it. What was going on inside me was somehow unconnected with my body. I sat quietly in my chair at the defense table each day—dressed in the shirt and tie and blazer that Bugliosi was so sure were for effect—sat with my Bible in front of me and my mouth sagging in an attempt to breathe. In the holding tank during recesses and before court started in the morning, I'd read that book, trying to draw out all the life that was in it for me.

Sometimes on days we weren't in court, Bubrick would bring my mother to visit me at the jail, but there was little I could say. She was hearing too much in court as it was, sitting almost motionless behind the dark glasses she always wore in case she wanted to cry. She never did cry in that courtroom, even with the enormity of what she heard. She saved her tears for nighttime in the squalid little room she'd rented in the Astor Apartments on Hill Street, within walking distance of the court in downtown Los Angeles. She didn't have access to a car, so each day she trekked to the court and every Sunday she'd walk several miles to a large Methodist church in the heart of the city. She never missed a Sunday, even though the minister made a point of ignoring her after her first visit, when she introduced herself in hopes he might give her some spiritual support and encouragement. "I guess city Methodists just aren't like country Methodists at home," she once said wistfully.

For someone who grew up on *Perry Mason* television dramas, the pace of an actual murder trial was excruciatingly slow. I did learn some things I had not known before, however. One was that in our orgy of death we'd missed the caretaker William Garretson, who was a few hundred feet away, across the swimming pool in a guest house listening to music while the slaughter went on. I had actually heard about him from one of my lawyers before the trial began, but now I saw him: a nervous, thin boy about my age. He avoided my eyes. I'm still amazed that he didn't hear the shots or Frykowski's screams for help, but as Bugliosi later said in his book, sounds did strange things in the canyons.

I also found out we'd missed almost a hundred dollars in cash in the Tate house, most of it in Jay Sebring's wallet, and I learned for the first time the full extent of our ferocity. Los Angeles County Coroner Thomas Noguchi laid it out carefully in his precise, high-pitched voice: Sharon Tate, stabbed sixteen times (any five of the wounds in and of themselves fatal); Abigail Folger, stabbed twenty-eight times; Voytek Frykowski, stabbed fifty-one times (seven of the wounds fatal), struck over the head with a blunt object thirteen times (the wounds collectively fatal), and shot twice. It went on and on, Deputy Medical Examiner David Katsuyama replacing Noguchi for descriptions of the LaBianca victims. I kept wondering how I could have, we could have, struck so many times. Later a defense psychiatrist, Dr. Ira Frank, would explain that speed sometimes creates a phenomenon called "preservation" — the mechanical repetition of a manual act or series of acts. That was how it had been, over and over, again and again, my arm like a machine, at one with the blade.

Dean Moorehouse made an appearance. I had not seen him since the day over three years before when he'd taken off for his second trial in Ukiah. He had not changed. When asked to state his occupation, he answered: "Turning people on to the truth." The former Methodist minister went on to say in his testimony that the more acid I'd taken the more and more beautiful a person I'd become. I wondered how beautiful Dean would have thought I was at 10050 Cielo Drive on August 9, or at 3301 Waverly Drive the following night.

Linda Kasabian was the star witness for the prosecution and she repeated the story she'd told at the trial of Charlie and the girls. It was the truth and it was horrible. My mother sat stiffly in the back of the courtroom, hearing the details for the first time. On her way down the corridor afterward, a photographer snapped her picture. She managed to get away before a reporter could ask her how it had felt to hear Linda's description of her son battering a man to death.

Later, my mother — along with Richard Carson and the onion farmer I'd worked for so many summers — testified about the kind of person I'd been before I left for California. Rich went on to say that once I'd joined the Family, I seemed to have lost my identity and any capacity for emotion.

Then I took the stand. Despite some of the truth I'd begun to see through reading the Bible and talking to Chaplain Goffigan, self-preservation won out in court and I admitted only what I felt I had to, what the prosecution already knew. I admitted shooting or stabbing everyone at the Tate house except Sharon. I denied killing her since Bugliosi and a previous jury were convinced Susan Atkins had done it. I claimed that Linda had driven to 10050 Cielo Drive, and tried to lay all the evidence of premeditation on Charlie or one of the girls. Also, since all the other witnesses to the events outside the LaBianca house had said that Charlie went in alone to tie up the victims, I went along with that story, figuring it made me look that much less responsible. I closed my testimony by saying that, at the time, the murders and the events around them had not seemed real to me, and that only since then had I developed an awareness of the reality of what I'd done and begun to feel remorse for it.

As both sides anticipated, the real focus of the trial was a battle between psychiatric experts as to whether or not I was insane. The defense called eight witnesses who testified that I was a paranoid schizophrenic (from intensive and chronic ingestion of drugs and hallucinogenics), that I had suffered organic brain damage, that my I. Q. had sunk from 120 to 89, that I was an insecure, dependent, immature personality type, and that I had been part of a *folie à deux* (a shared madness between two or more intimately related people). The witnesses all spoke with absolute assurance and presented various medical, neurological, and psychiatric tests to prove that I was insane and therefore not truly responsible for what I had done.

The prosecution had its own slate of expert psychologists, psychiatrists, and neurosurgeons. They were equally certain that I was either faking mental illness or suffering a psychological disturbance that was not so severe as to render me unable to commit deliberate, premeditated murder and know what it meant, morally and legally. There was no doubt, they said, that under the law I was fully responsible for what I had done on those two nights.

The jury believed Mr. Bugliosi's experts, but apparently Judge Alexander found ours more convincing. As Bugliosi later complained, the judge did show enormous skepticism toward the prosecution witnesses and equally obvious confidence in ours, and he did say, on the day I was sentenced, that if he had tried the case without a jury, he would possibly have arrived at a different verdict.

Long before the trial ended, I was quite certain that I would be convicted (though somehow I didn't think I would be sentenced to death). Bubrick must have also felt we were fighting a losing battle, since in his summation he suddenly resurrected a theory which the girls had tried to use in the earlier trial. He accused poor Linda Kasabian of being the primary culprit, the real ringleader who directed the murders at Cielo Drive and was rewarded for her success by driving the car the next night. It was patently ridiculous, but Bubrick closed his remarks by, pointing out that while I was in high school "back in Texas playing football, what was Linda Kasabian doing? She was going from commune to commune, traveling from man to man, living off boyfriends, shooting speed, selling drugs, living by her wits." The jury still found her testimony compelling — and on October 12, 1971, found me guilty of seven counts of first-degree murder and one count of conspiracy to commit murder.

The sanity phase of the trial was short, and the verdict a foregone conclusion. On October 19, after only two and a half hours of deliberation, the jury decided I was sane when the murders were committed.

On October 21, it took them six hours to determine that I deserved the death penalty. It had begun with music and love in a Sunset Boulevard mansion and now it would end with Charlie and me together again on San Quentin's Death Row.

Lockup

Death Row has a terrible and final ring to it, but by the time I arrived at San Quentin in November 1971, there was already talk that the California Supreme Court would strike down the death penalty in the state as "cruel and unusual punishment." The gas chamber at Quentin hadn't been used in years, and the consensus on the Row said that "the man ain't gonna drop the pill no more."

By now I was used to prison life and was stronger, physically and psychologically. It was as if each day I found a little more of the self that I'd worked so hard to destroy. Each day a little more of the humanity I'd trampled down inside me came back to life.

I spent a lot of my time reading the Scriptures and that, more than anything else, seemed to nourish the human part of me that was being reborn. I believed that God had His hand on me, that He was with me, and I was certain He'd forgiven me all the evil I'd brought down on myself and the world around me. I'd recognized the depth of my sin; I admitted it as best I could and repented with a remorse that grew as my wholeness grew — like nerve endings being restored in a burn, the pain a sign of healing. I knew I could trust that all I had been and still was could be made new-because God had reached out to me across the gap my sin had created between us and wiped away my guilt — not cheaply, but at the cost of the life of His own Son, blood for blood, life for life.

But there was something incomplete about it all. It was real, but somehow it seemed unfinished. I know now the problem was simply that I still saw my relationship with God in terms of what He was giving me — forgiveness, comfort, healing in my mind — and not what I should be giving Him — my whole self and all rights to it. I wanted a Savior very much, but I wasn't ready for a Lord.

Prisoners on Death Row were not allowed in the yard except to go to the dentist or the infirmary, but I settled into the confined life we had together on the tier as well as could be expected, watching eagerly for the few days of the year when we'd get sunlight from the high windows across the walkway. We were a peculiar community — all of us technically waiting to die, all judged guilty of capital crimes. For all the sin and agony and violence that we represented, we lived a surprisingly mundane life. Some men passed their time playing dominos, lifting weights, studying correspondence courses or, that perennial favorite, working on legal appeals. Or one could read as I did or watch the televisions that were suspended above the walkway, one for every three men. Even though we were fed separately in our cells, between ten and two every day we were allowed out on the tier to talk and exercise. In that holding tank for the legally doomed, I made my first feeble attempts at reaching out again to the human beings around me. Another part of me began to heal.

When I wasn't reading my Bible (it was already beginning to look worn), I wrote letters. From the time I'd left Texas until my release from Atascadero I'd never corresponded with anyone, even my parents, but sometime before my mother came out for the trial I started attempting short notes to the two of them. By the time I reached San Quentin, I had a long list of people to write to: family, friends, Bill Boyd (I kept pestering him for legal advice and with suggestions for appeal tactics), and one special, rather strange girl I'd met during the trial. I'll call her Freda Hofmann.

It takes a very unique personality to decide to fall in love with a man in prison, especially one sentenced to death. Freda apparently had that sort of personality. She was in Los Angeles on a visa from Germany when my trial began and for some reason she started coming to it. I noticed her in court several times—a dark, attractive girl with a certain sense of distance toward the people surrounding her. In the crowded courtroom, her face seemed to stand out; there was a kind of wall around her that cut her off from the rest of the crowd. Maybe it was just that her attention always stayed focused totally on me.

Suddenly she stopped coming (I found out later she lost her passport and couldn't be admitted, since identification was required). I pretty much forgot about her until several days later when she started showing up in the halls and elevators of the courthouse, never saying anything, just looking at me and smiling. I wasn't getting too many smiles at that point so I started smiling back and waving to her. The television cameras picked it up and suddenly Freda was established as my girlfriend before we'd ever spoken to one another.

One day a note arrived for me at the county jail, and after that we wrote brief letters to each other occasionally. About the time I was sent to Death Row, she went back to Germany, but we continued to correspond. She would send me pictures and clippings and kept talking about coming back to America to see me again. At first I wondered if she had an ulterior motive — a book or some kind of exclusive article — but finally I accepted the fact that although we'd never spent any time together, she liked me.

All the speculation about the Supreme Court's decision on the death penalty was ended on February 18, 1972, when that penalty was declared to be in violation of the state constitution's ban on cruel and unusual punishment. We'd been told it was coming and the whole Row waited up that night until the news came out on television. There wasn't any cheering but you could feel the relief. The threat of death was gone — and no matter how the law might be changed in the future, we would never again face that small room and the cyanide tablet. Death Row had only been my home for a few months, but for some of the others it was a matter of years. Now the place was a legal anachronism.

It wasn't until August, however, that I was transferred into the general prison population. After the isolation and sense of security of the Row, the yard was a frightening place with its exposure and potential violence. Drugs were passed openly and rumors and threats were daily bread. I got a job in the prison furniture factory and had barely gotten into the work when I was notified a month later that I was to be moved to the California Men's Colony outside of San Luis Obispo. The Department of Corrections wanted to get me away from the other Manson people at San Quentin.

The move was one of the best things that ever happened to me. In a state with an above-average prison system, the Colony is the most progressive and well-run institution of the lot. The level of violence is extremely low, and the staff is generally professional and compassionate. The prison itself looked like a resort the first time I saw it, riding up in the bus on September 19, 1972: green hills rising up beyond the quads, special trailers for family and conjugal visits, lawns and flowers and open spaces and light and air. And there was also a Protestant chaplain by the name of Stanley McGuire, though I wouldn't come to appreciate him immediately.

In place of the cells I'd been used to for the past three years, the Men's Colony had small separate rooms with inmates holding their own keys (doors are automatically locked at night). There was a freedom of movement that seemed unbelievable to me after Los Angeles and the Row — only someone who's been without it can appreciate the luxury of letting sunlight fall on your face.

I was placed in Building #7, a unit for psychiatric cases, and put to work in the dining room. Eventually I found a much better job in the psychiatric department as a clerk. I kept records, made labels, and arranged distribution of medication from the pharmacy that was beyond a locked door just behind my work area. I never had access to the drugs themselves, and my superiors liked me and trusted me, but in late spring of the next year the San Francisco Chronicle ran an article stating that Charles "Tex" Watson, the drug-crazed Manson killer, was handing out dangerous drugs in his job at the California Men's Colony. The article was based on a misunderstanding of my work, but pretty soon a directive came down from the head of the Department of Corrections that I was to be moved. I ended up as clerk for the head psychiatric nurse.

It is the generally held opinion of inmates and staff alike (except for the staffs of psychiatric units) that most of the psychological work done in prisons is a waste of time and money. Despite the occasional case of real help and improvement for a particular individual, the psychiatric system as it presently exists within correctional institutions is a classic example of man's trying to solve his moral and ethical and spiritual problems (which modern thinking likes to tag "psychological" because it sounds more scientific) without turning to the only real Source of moral and spiritual renewal. To put it more positively, I am convinced that only Jesus Christ can rehabilitate men and women who, for whatever complex of reasons, have made choices that led them into crime. Even those who do not share my view of the answer admit that the problem exists, however.

The prisoner is caught in a bind. Attendance at group therapy and active participation in whatever "game" the psychologist may come up with are imperative, because such participation is necessary for a good board report when you come up for parole. Thus, by his participation, the prisoner is blackmailed into supporting and helping to maintain a bureaucratic system that does little or nothing for him. Not surprisingly, cynicism is widespread among inmates, and even the newest and most naive prisoner soon learns the particular jargon and poses that will get him a good report from his shrink.

It didn't take me long to figure out how to play the game. I spent three and a half years in group therapy with a psychologist who was eventually fired from the staff for supplying some prisoners with drugs in exchange for sex. Obviously this one experience, or even the general attitude of one institution, should not write off the efforts of a whole profession, but I believe that until we admit the spiritual roots of many of our so-called psychological problems, we will never change the present patterns of recidivism that our penal system produces.

Over the next two years, my life at the Colony settled into something probably as comfortable as prison life can ever be. Along with having a job I liked, I'd started making wooden toys and hobby crafts after an old man across the hall loaned me some tools. I was good at it and ended up with a huge tool chest and a long stream of projects for my family and friends. There was something very good about using my hands again to build things and make them perfect down to the last detail.

Along with my work, there was Freda. Shortly after I was transferred down to the Colony I wrote to her in Germany and mentioned that the visiting situation here was much better than it had been at any other institution-a lounge with sofas and chairs and the opportunity for real conversation and even physical contact. A month or two later she flew back from Germany and got an apartment in Los Angeles. Every weekend she'd hitchhike the two hundred and some miles up the coast to visit me. When her visa expired, she went back to Europe for a short time but then returned with a lifetime visa and the idea of marrying me, even though I was serving a life sentence. Whatever I thought of the marriage plans, it felt good to have somebody to love.

If Freda's company wasn't enough, my parents flew out and spent a week with me each year, the three of us staying together in one of the trailers on the grounds, almost like a normal family.

Everything was good. Maybe too good. Shortly after I was transferred to the Colony I stopped reading my

Bible and praying. Perhaps it had all just been "jailhouse religion," after all. I didn't really care whether it was or not. All I cared about was making my life as comfortable as possible as long as I had to be in — and finding a legal approach to get me out.

Every one of my parents' letters closed with a paragraph of spiritual counsel that I came to call "The Jesus Letter" and never read. When Bill Boyd suggested in one of his notes that I consider memorizing Scripture, I thought he'd gone crazy. Unless he could spring me, I was too busy with work and the toys and Freda and plans for a new appeal to think too much about God. The vision in the hospital room that had seemed to be such a turning point started to fade into the rest of my past, just one more fragment of unrelated dreaming-done, finished with.

But God refused to be put off so easily.

Day

This is the chapter I've been waiting for . . . .

The last reference to me in Prosecutor Bugliosi's *Helter Skelter* has me off the Row and no longer "playing insane," with a "girl friend who visits him regularly." That was 1974, and except for the fact that I had never been playing insane, the statement pretty much says it. But *Helter Skelter* was not the last word. Even if I wanted to forget that moment when out of the void and darkness around me the light and love of Christ reached out to me, God was not going to forget it. He was going to see that what He had begun in me was completed, as was promised in Philippians 1:6.

Late in 1974 it seemed that everything started going stale. My job in the psychiatric unit wasn't interesting anymore, the future stretched out to nothing, going nowhere, and even my relationship with Freda seemed to have run its course. She still visited me every weekend, but we were strained with each other, falling back on habit, and trying to avoid the fact that we had nothing more to say to each other. At the time I couldn't explain what was happening to me, but now I realize that it was the Lord — as that great Christian Saint Augustine said: ". . . the heart of man is restless until it finds its rest in Thee." Augustine knew what he was talking about; he'd spent a lot of years running from God himself, just as I had. But it was time to stop running and face the inescapable love that was being poured down on me in spite of my disinterest, in spite of all I'd been and done.

I had no way of knowing it then, but hundreds of people across the country were praying for me at this time, not just my family and the little church in Copeville, but all kinds of brothers and sisters whom God touched with a concern for me. I know now that all good comes from the Lord, but I will always be grateful to those people as well, many that I'll never even know about in this life, who were willing to trust the shocking promise of God that there is no soul so corrupted that His grace can't heal it and make it new.

Their faith in the face of what would seem so obvious to the world — that someone like Tex Watson was beyond hope — was the instrument of God's full salvation in my life and I praise Him for it.

I cling to that same hope when I remember Charlie and all the others each day in my prayers. I know that idea may shock some, even some Christians, but the Word of God makes it clear that even Manson is a creation of the Father — no matter how hard he tried to turn himself into the incarnation of Satan — and that God loves and waits for him, just as the father of the prodigal son waited each day on the road, hoping to see his son come back to him (see Luke 15:11 ff.). I know most ordinary people can't help but be so frightened and horrified by

Manson and the crimes that Charlie almost ceases to seem human to them, but the grace of God calls us to become more than ordinary people, to see things as He sees them. I'm convinced that God sees Charles Manson's acts, what he created in himself and in us to spill over into the world in death, as the stench of the very Bottomless Pit which Charlie was hoping to find. But I'm just as convinced that God looks on Charlie himself, even seeing all that he is, and loves him, and would send His Son to the cross for him alone, as He would (and in a sense did) for every one of us. When I pray for Charlie, I have no doubt I'm praying at one with the will of my Father in heaven, at one with the love of Jesus who gave Himself for Charlie Manson, as for every other man, woman, and child on God's earth. But I'm getting ahead of myself.

One Saturday, as 1974 was dragging to an end, I overheard a conversation in the visiting room while I was with Freda. A girl was sharing Jesus with a buddy of mine who sat near us. As she went on, I couldn't stop listening. There was a life and a spirit in her, a real excitement as she talked about giving everything over to Christ — not just her problems and needs, but all she had and was — and making it her only purpose to serve and follow Him wherever He led her. Even when I'd been reading the Bible every day and trying to pray, I'd never had the kind of intimate, loving relationship with Christ that she was talking about.

Freda had had a bad experience with her religious upbringing as a child, and she got very annoyed when I tried to join in the conversation. Religion, she said, was for idiots — a crutch. I wasn't so sure. Something about what I'd seen in that other girl, pouring out her love so simply and so beautifully there in the visiting room, stayed with me and kept me thinking.

The fantastic thing about God's sovereignty — when it's something you experience and not a theological principle you argue about — is seeing how He can draw together a dozen different separate events to achieve His purpose, without any individual part necessarily being aware of how it fits into the larger plan of the Father.

Shortly after hearing that conversation in the visiting room, I got a letter from Chico Holiday, an evangelist who has had a unique ministry to prisoners, due to his own powerful personal testimony of how God touched his life. I'd never heard of this man with the funny name, and I had no way of knowing that my mother had written to him earlier and asked him to contact me. (His first reaction was that her letter was a hoax, but he stepped out in faith and wrote to me anyway). He'd sent two of his books along, so I decided I might as well read them. Time is one thing you have plenty of, with a life sentence.

By the time I was partway through the first of the books, I felt something drawing me to the prison chapel. I'd never gone to any services since I'd come to the Colony, never had any dealings with the men who were part of the program, but now I felt like a hungry man who hears

233

there's dinner being served down the street — he has to go and see what he can get. I had to go to the chapel, even if I couldn't quite explain why.

I don't know how much I got out of those first services, sitting quietly in the back, feeling the eyes on me. Like any closed community, a prison has an enormous amount of gossip, and I was a prisoner lots of people knew about. Now word got around that the guy who'd killed the Tate woman was sitting in chapel.

I'll always be thankful that the Lord saw fit to show His love to me not only through people from "outside" but through solid Christian brothers right here in the prison — men like Phil Alleman and Joe Talley — fellow inmates who had given themselves to Him and who started sharing with me and supporting me, from the moment I set foot in that chapel. As much as anything else, it was their quiet, consistent love and witness — never pushing themselves on me, never trying to force the issue — that made me want to keep coming back, made me feel that somewhere inside me there was an emptiness that what they had could fill.

I continued to correspond with Chico Holiday, and then in January 1975, a Christian musical group called Psalm 150 appeared in a chapel program. They took their name from the last of the Hebrew Psalms, which includes the words: "Praise him with blasts of trumpets. Praise him with lyre and harp. Praise him with drums and dancing, with strings and reeds, with cymbals" (see vv. 3-5). That pretty much described their music and their ministry.

When I'd been with Charlie I'd thought music spoke to me — his and the Beatles' — and now here was music that seemed to talk right into my head. But the message was so much different: no Helter Skelter, no death. This message talked about the life that was waiting to explode inside me if I'd just give myself to it.

But I held back, because by now I realized that if I really said yes to this, it couldn't be what it had been before — just giving God my problems and asking Him to spring me from the joint, and trying to do a little better in the way I lived.

This time I'd have to go the whole shot: I'd have to admit that God really had made me, that His Son's death was all that would remake the mess I'd made of myself. My admission of that meant the only possible response was to give myself totally to Him, really let Him be God to me, let Him be the whole of my being, the only ultimately important thing, the focus and reason for my living each day.

I tried to hedge. I'd think about it, I told myself, *I'd work into it gradually*. But every time I'd go into the chapel, every time one of the Christian inmates would share with me, so lovingly and so gently, I wanted more and more to have what they were experiencing — the peace and assurance that come from knowing that whatever happens to you is all right because you can glorify God in it and that's all that really matters anyway.

It was at this same time that God brought a man by the name of Ray Hoekstra into my life, "Chaplain Ray" to the millions of people who listen to his radio broadcasts and have been touched by his ministry. I didn't know much about him except that the Lord had given him a special work among prison inmates and correctional officials. When he asked to see me, I was wondering in the back of my mind if he had something he wanted out of me — a famous convert maybe, somebody from whom he could gain some publicity.

It was hard to keep thinking that way after I met him. He was a fellow Texan in his fifties, and that Texas accent and his direct, open smile did a lot to lower my defenses. Most of all there was the fact that he seemed totally untouched by what he knew I'd been. It wasn't that he didn't take my crimes seriously — he obviously did — but that they didn't affect in any way the fact of his loving me, of his wanting to tell me some great news that he was so excited about he was sure I couldn't help but be excited too: the news that whatever I'd done could be completely washed away and forgiven in God's eyes, and I could start the rest of my life fresh and whole and clean as a newborn child. God loved me — he made no bones about it. Just as it was with the prisoners in the chapel, the fact that Chaplain Ray so obviously loved me, too, and that Jesus loved me through him, was more convincing than all the words he could have said.

Chaplain Ray also brought me some startling information: Susan Atkins — the Sadie who'd shocked even me when I first came to the Family with her wild life and lack of inhibitions, who'd talked about killing being like a sexual release — Susan Atkins had found this forgiveness and rebirth that he was talking about. So had Bruce Davis, who'd screamed down messages from Charlie in the L.A. jail until I'd felt I could never escape his voice again. Bruce and Sadie—now they were part of what I'd seen in the brothers in the chapel, in the young singers and instrumentalists in Psalm 150, in this heavyset, good-natured Texan with the glasses and unembarrassed smile.

The chaplain and I have become good friends since that day (obviously, since he ended up being the one to whom I'd tell my story for this book), but at that point I still wasn't ready, as much as a part of myself wanted to say yes to what he was talking about. I had given myself totally once before, to Charlie, and even though I knew this was something completely different — even though I understood what Chaplain Ray meant when he told me that as we give ourselves to Christ He doesn't annihilate us, but rather rebuilds us and remakes us into what we were created to be in the first place — I was still afraid.

I kept on going to the chapel, and during the last week of May there was a revival. I know that's a term that makes a lot of people uncomfortable nowadays, so maybe it would be better to call it a time of intensive sharing of the Good News that these Christian men in the prison were living out every day. I attended every night and, after the first of the services, when a student chaplain asked all who wanted to take what God was offering to raise their hands, I slipped mine up, as inconspicuously as possible. But I wasn't ready to walk down to the front with all those men watching me, to admit in front of them all that I was dying inside, desperately hungry for the life and spiritual food that I saw all around me in the Christian brothers who had witnessed to me. I went back to my room torn apart.

Finally, on June 1, the last night of the special services, I decided that this had to be it; I couldn't play games any longer. I understood very clearly what was being offered: God who made us, God from whom we'd turned away to follow our own selfishness, God who wanted us back as His sons and daughters, wanted *me* back. To bridge the gap between us, He'd sent His own Son to take our death — the inevitable consequence of our sin — on Himself. That had not only opened up an eternity of fellowship with our Creator in this life and the next, it made positive change and renewal possible in our lives right now, in *my* life right now. It began a process of slowly becoming the whole person one was born to be, of becoming more and more like Christ Himself. It wasn't just a fire escape — that actually had very little to do with it — it was letting ourselves be participants in a total victory over evil and death that was already won because Christ had risen from the dead. It was deciding that His Kingdom and His will for us were the only things that really mattered. Having decided to give Him our whole lives, we are to let the mighty Spirit of God come into our own spirits to start building the life of Christ in us, and to enable us to do the service to which we are called.

That is what it is all about, I thought as I sat in the back of the chapel on that last night, sensing that the Reverend DeVito was reaching the end of his sermon. It occurred to me suddenly that to make this step would mean giving up even that most precious thing I had: the determination to somehow find the legal machinery that would get me out of prison and back into the world. It would mean, if that was God's will, accepting a natural life that never extended beyond the walls of the Colony; it would mean asking for nothing except to be used or even set aside for the glory of God. It would mean all that and more. When the invitation was given, I ran to the front.

I was baptized by one of the student chaplains fifteen days later, in a large plastic laundry cart in the garden outside the chapel. It was big enough for me to go completely under the water and die there with Christ. No matter how silly it might have looked to someone from the outside, someone who didn't understand all that was going on in that moment, to me it was as glorious as the River Jordan where John washed people in preparation for the coming of the Messiah. My Messiah had come, at last; He had come to me and I was His. As I burst up out of the water and it splattered off me like liquid fire in the sunlight, I felt all that horror and guilt that was rightfully mine splash away with it, all the weight of what I had done and been. That night two weeks before when I'd stumbled forward in the chapel, I'd finally had a full realization of exactly what I had done, a realization so devastating that all I had been able to do was weep for what seemed like hours. Now that burden was lifted; I would weep again, many times, for those I'd hurt — the dead and the living — but from now on it would be tears shed in the certainty that the punishment for that hurt had been taken and the debt paid — not by me, but by God Himself. If that sounds like unmerited grace, I suppose it always is so for us, but for God the cost was immeasurable. Who are we to reject His gift because we can never pay for it? That's what a gift is all about-a free, spontaneous act of love.

Paul wrote in a letter to the squalid, backbiting, sin-filled church at Corinth:

Therefore, if any one is in Christ, he is a new creation; the old has passed away, behold the new has come. 2 Corinthians 5:17 RSV

That's how God sees it. We live it as a process and a promise. I can only be grateful that I was permitted by my wise Heavenly Father to begin that process in the midst of the body of believers at the Plazaview Chapel in the Colony, because it is like no other prison chapel in the country.

To Live is Christ

When the Reverend Stanley McGuire came to California Men's Colony as Protestant chaplain in 1967 — the same year I was leaving Texas for California — he had a vision for a different kind of prison ministry.

Traditionally, prison chaplaincies have been like a lot of missionary outreach activities to the Third World: colonialistic. That is, many a chaplain has never worked himself out of a job by building an actual, self-sustaining, organic church — a true "body of Christ" that ministers to and governs and disciplines itself. The traditional view has assumed that convicts (or people from less advanced cultures) can never be anything more than babes in Christ, saved by the grace of God but kept in perpetual spiritual infancy. They are not to be trusted to mature and function together as a gathered company of believers without the supervision and control of an outsider, be it a chaplain or a white missionary.

Stanley McGuire did not share this traditional position. Looking to the New Testament, he saw that God's intent in redeeming men and women was to have them personally grow and mature in Him — not just "get saved" and stop there — and also to build together a living organism that would be a vehicle for Christ's Spirit to minister to the members through the members and bear witness to the world in which they found themselves.

Chaplain McGuire decided that, according to the Word of God, a redeemed sinner is a redeemed sinner whether he happens to be behind bars or on the outside, and if those on the outside could be trusted — by the grace and transforming power of Christ—to grow and build up the church, the same was true of the Christian convict, even if he was still incarcerated.

If the Scriptures are correct when they say that "the old has passed away" for the new, growing Christian, McGuire reasoned, then there is absolutely no difference between the spiritual status of a Christian brother or sister in jail and one outside. To assume otherwise and to treat prisoners as a special class within the church was the worst kind of spiritual pride. It said, if not in words, that some sins are worse than others (at least getting caught at them is) and therefore some sinners are worse than others, less trustworthy after they have been touched by grace. This was obviously in direct conflict with the teaching of the Bible, which says that all sin is equally damaging to our relationship with God (James 2:10) and all sinners equally eligible for redemption (1 John 1:8-10). Chaplain McGuire also noted that many of the first apostolic churches were made up not of the conventionally virtuous, but of redeemed prostitutes, murderers, thieves, extortionists, and outlaws—the very people who make up a prison chapel—and that these early Christians had managed to become great saints and witnesses for their Lord (1 Corinthians 6:9-11).

Stanley McGuire decided that the same thing could happen at California Men's Colony — he would make it happen by building a New Testament church among the men, a real body of growing, mutually sustaining believers in Jesus Christ.

By the time I became a part of the chapel program in June 1975, this had happened. Prisoners were deacons, counselors, preachers, liturgists and teachers. It was their own church and they, submitting to the Spirit of God, functioned like any body of Jesus' disciples — not always perfectly, but as growing Christian men not spiritual parasites.

Strangely, in some ways it is easier to admit my sins than it is to try to talk about what God has chosen, in His love, to do through me and in me in the past two years. With the guidance and prayers of my brothers here—as well as the support of many men and women outside these walls—I've been able to not only grow in Christ but serve Him as well.

Within the Plazaview Chapel community our life together as a gathered body of Christians-and my life as a part of that body — has only one goal: to bring glory to our Lord Jesus Christ. Strengthened by the Spirit of God Himself, we attempt to accomplish this through mutual support of each individual brother's growth and vocation in Christ, through the offering of our praise and worship and through witness to those around us, inmates and officers alike. Not just by the testimony of our words, but by the quality of our lives, we hope to make it clear to anyone who is interested that Jesus Christ is Lord, not only of Creation, but of our individual lives, that He forgives and restores and redeems anyone who turns to Him.

When I became a part of this community, this local church in the Men's Colony, I discovered I was desperately hungry for spiritual food: the presence and Word of my newfound Lord. The Bible that I had ignored in my childhood and stumbled through half-blind as I began my slow struggle back to humanity in the Los Angeles County Jail—the Bible that had for so long seemed a black-bound irrelevancy or a club in my parents' hands — that Bible suddenly opened itself to me with new and shattering power.

The Word of God began to make direct and inescapable sense to me because it talked about death and life, enslavement and liberation, sin and righteousness. These things were my own story, a story now seen and understood clearly for the first time. The promises it made — forgiveness, renewal, and the power of the Holy Spirit of God Himself falling on and filling ordinary, rebellious men and women and turning them into mighty witnesses for God-those promises were no longer pious dreams. They were the reality I was beginning to live each day along with my brothers around me. As the Book of Acts described the life of the earliest Christian community in Jerusalem in the years just after the Resurrection, it could have been describing what we were living, day by day. We saw the same miracles: broken lives put back together, hatred and violence turned to love, the power of physical addictions and perversities broken, sickness made well. We experienced the same love that binds brother to brother in support and fellowship. We knew the same life-giving power in the gifts of the Spirit through which God spoke and ministered directly to us and through us. God's Word, especially the New Testament, formed us as it described us. It became, as one of the scriptural writers puts it, a living Word.

Our fellowship together was equally important. It was (and is) not a matter of simply coming together once a week out of custom or to listen to a lecture or to have religious "entertainment" or a reason to see friends. Our varying times together each day, times of instruction, prayer, praise, and ministry to each other, remain the vital lifeblood of our individual spiritual growth, the source of our life together as a body of Christians and the power for our outreach into the sometimes hostile prison world around us.

My first responsibility within the Plazaview Chapel community was serving as worship clerk for the Sunday interdenominational services. As I became more involved and committed to the work and shared life of our church, I was appointed a deacon. It was while I was serving as senior deacon two years ago that I began to think a great deal about just how those of us in the Plazaview community could reach out to the desperately needy, broken prison population around us, a population that at least conventional morality would see as the most self-evident "fallen" in all our world. It was not enough for us to nourish and support each other through our prayers and our fellowship, nor was it enough to try to live straight lives in the quads and tiers that were our home at Men's Colony. It was not even enough to share the Good News of what Jesus Christ offered in Himself to people who came to us with problems or spiritual hunger.

I came to see that we could not stand apart and wait for people to come to us. If we were to be like Jesus our Lord, we had to reach out in caring and healing to the world around us, throw ourselves into it willingly and with real love, just as He did. We must offer ourselves to their needs with genuine concern for them, not just a desire to get people to agree with us. It wouldn't do any good to try to shove Jesus down people's throats, I was sure of that. Too many men in prison have already had too much "religion" pushed at them by well-meaning do-gooders. But I became convinced that in prison, just as out, people are susceptible to genuine love that starts with them, their own concerns and struggles, however individual. Love was what the sometimes hardened, cynical men around us needed and, whether they would admit it or not, love was what they wanted. Most important, love was what Christ would give them first if He were locked up with them, just as it was what He gave to the people who came to Him during His life among us. Now we were Christ — Christ to and for the world around us at the Men's Colony. Christ lived in us by His Spirit and He could love through us. I shared my vision with the other deacons and they were equally excited by the idea: a vigorous program of outreach and witness that started not with a desire to force people to accept what you said, what you believed, and had experienced, but rather a program that started with a desire to love and serve people, as Christ loves and gives Himself for them, just as they are.

It began to have effect — not overnight, not all at once, and not without setbacks and rejections and disappointments, but we have seen tremendous growth in the past two years. As we have laid ourselves and our love on the line for those around us — seeking them out in the quads and on the fields and in their rooms, not to preach to them but to find ways we can help them, ways we can offer ourselves to them in Christ's love—the real spiritual needs have time and again come out, and the answer to those needs has been spoken and received: Jesus, alive in His world through men and women who belong to Him.

In the past two years my own experience in my God has deepened as well and — surprising as it may sound to some — I have come to understand that His call for me is to training and preparation for ordained ministry within the church of Christ's redeemed people. Through an excellent student-chaplaincy program that Chaplain McGuire has developed, others within the Chapel community and I are given extensive preparation and study (a process I'm still in the midst of as this is being written) as well as practical experience of leadership in our own local church in the prison.

My life is very full — sometimes almost too full, it seems, when I have to wait for days to find time to write a letter. I spend at least an hour each day visiting inmates in my quad in the outreach program I've already described. Sometimes a visit may mean nothing more than a hello or supplying the inmate with greeting cards, writing supplies, or a dictionary; sometimes it may mean serious counseling and prayer together in the room. Whatever good comes of it — and a great deal does — is not my doing. It is God's Spirit who moves in men's lives to change and heal them. I can only bear witness, live out my witness as best I can, and give the result over the God. It is His work anyway, not mine.

As a student chaplain and also associate administrator for the Plazaview Chapel program (as I noted earlier, Chaplain McGuire means business when he talks about an inmate-run church), I have a small office just off the sanctuary of our Protestant chapel. It's there that a lot of my study goes on (approximately six hours a day), as well as further counseling.

Since the goal of the program, as of every authentic Christian community, is to develop discipleship — spiritual maturity and a genuinely and increasingly Christ-like life — instruction for new believers is an important part of the program, and I teach one weekly class for new Christians. My time with these twenty or so new brothers is one of the highlights of each week.

As part of my responsibilities as a student chaplain, I preach several times each month, celebrate the Communion, baptize, and lead in worship in our more structured Sunday-morning services. During the week, in less formal times of prayer and praise, I lead one of several Bible-study groups in the program and participate with my brothers in times of free worship and sharing in the powerfully present and guiding Spirit of Jesus.

Since the prison environment — just like the world outside — has enormous negative spiritual resources for attacking a new believer, we have an active program of "shepherding" for new Christians that provides each new believer with a more mature brother who accepts personal responsibility for support, counsel, and encouragement. As I look back on my own so-called decision for Christ as a child in the local church in Copeville, after which it was assumed that I was "taken care of," now that I'd been baptized, I can only wish that more churches outside prison walls would take seriously their responsibility for young (not necessarily in calendar years) converts and the struggles and discouragements they must inevitably face. "You are not alone" is the most important thing a new Christian needs to know, and the shepherding program assures this knowledge, reminding the new believer that now not only Christ stands by him; fellow believers are also with him to encourage and support him, even at times to hold him accountable.

Perhaps the two most beautiful times of each day are the times spent with some of my brothers in prayer and openness before the Lord. The Old Testament Psalmist was constantly writing about how good it was to praise and bless the Lord, and I know it's true. It only makes me sad that, for so many Christians today, coming together for worship has become a sterile exercise in patient listening and unthinking form. It is good to praise the One who made and remakes and in the end will transform us into something more glorious than we can even begin to imagine.

At the Men's Colony I experience just how good it is to praise and pray to my God when, during each noon hour, Charlie Kerrigan and Claudie Conover (the two fellow Student Chaplains who have been so important in my own Christian walk) join me in my office for an hour of worship and intercession, and again each evening when the brothers from my quad join in the sometimes dark and sometimes cold and sometimes rain on the bleachers of our quad's athletic field for a time of intercessory prayer.

Each night we lift up each other and our needs, the needs of those around us in the prison, and requests for prayer from friends and family outside. There is much to pray for at the Men's Colony, where God's creatures are trapped in patterns of violence and hatred and vengeance, men are tormented by addictions and twisted sexual drives, and new believers are caught in the peer pressure of their anti-Christian environment. But there is also much to pray for in the world outside our walls. There are friends who write to us with aching hearts for people they love, torn by all the same death and darkness we see on the inside. Each night we come before our wise, loving Heavenly Father in the name of His Son, knowing that He hears and that His will will be accomplished. We are only grateful that in His great love He allows us to be a part of the working out of that divine purpose through our faithful prayers.

We may be behind prison walls and electric fences (and justly so), but in Jesus Christ, we are free. Thanks be to God for His indescribable love. We have known it. We live it. It is real.

What of the future? It would be foolish for any man who is in prison to try to claim he has no interest in whether or not he ever gets out. Outside is always better than in, even at as good an institution as Men's Colony. But I can say this truthfully: All I ultimately care about is serving the God who was willing to give Himself for me, to reach down and draw me out of the living death I'd made for myself. If I can serve Him better in prison, so be it. If I can serve Him better outside, then I will wait for Him to put me where He wants me.

Whatever happens, I do not think that what God has done for me somehow entitles me to any sort of special treatment or early release, and I would never desecrate the gift of His love and redemption by trying to use it to get some kind of legal advantage for myself.

As Paul said, "I am not my own property; I have been bought and paid for" (see 1 Corinthians 6:20). *And at such a great price: the life of my Lord.* I would be a fool to try to claim any rights over what belongs to Him, not to me. I can be happy wherever He allows me to be, because my happiness, my joy, and my life are in Him — and He is everywhere.

The rebirth that has taken place in me has happened to millions of God's children over the past two thousand years. It is not unique to me or a few like me. It is happening today, right now, as you read this. Everywhere you go, you pass men and women who live it as I do.

It is sadly ironic that what makes my story more "interesting" than theirs is not the light we share but the darkness I knew before it. In one sense, all that darkness no longer exists for me; its spiritual power is gone, nailed to the cross with Jesus. I have dragged it all out again, in more detail than ever, only in the hope that those who learn the truth of that darkness will take more seriously the reality of the light that is there for them, too — and for *you*, if you ask for it.

For the pain that any retelling of some of these events must cause the families of the victims or my own family, I can only pray that God will ease the burden with His love. I hope the greater truth, the fact of just how encompassing God's power to bring new life can be — evidenced in what He's done in me — will be what lasts in readers' hearts and minds. I also hope that those who lost family and friends they loved because of me will be able to find the strength to forgive, somewhere within their broken hearts.

The questions *Why?* and *How?* won't go away. Bugliosi ends his book on those questions, suggesting that Charlie's use of sex and drugs and fantasy, of isolation and fear and religion, even his use of real, though misdirected, love all worked together to give him his peculiar control over those of us who were finally willing to go out into the night and kill innocent strangers on his orders. But Prosecutor Bugliosi admits that there must have been "something more," though he is at a loss to explain what it is. My answer may not please the prosecutor or the skeptics, but I lived it and I think Charlie was—perhaps still is—possessed.

How it happened and when it happened, I have no way of knowing. Perhaps a frightened, tormented boy — passed from a prostitute mother to various unfeeling relatives and spending seventeen years in prison before he was thirty — made a deliberate choice at some point, inviting the demonic forces into himself. Or perhaps they came uninvited, in the guise of his anger and hostility and desperate need to be something, anything, even Satan if that was all there was. However it happened, I'm convinced it was true, that those of us who were touched by Charlie, who opened ourselves to him, opened ourselves to a larger presence, a deeper darkness than just his twisted soul.

I do not mean by this that he was not responsible for the monstrous horrors he created, or that this somehow places him out of the bounds of God's redeeming love, either. I simply offer it as an explanation for the "something more" that Bugliosi sensed but could not define. Perhaps if we took the spiritual powers of evil in our world more seriously, we might see more clearly both the reality of and the solution for all our evil and sin, seen and unseen.

Whatever spiritual forces were at work in Charlie, however, he did not create the materials of his bizarre theories and lifestyle out of nothing. The raw materials were all there. In a real sense, he simply took the rhetoric and the symbols of the sixties counterculture — at least its radical edge — and gave them flesh, translated them into life.

Charlie was not the first to label the establishment as pigs. And while the Beatles may not have been speaking to him directly, there is little doubt that the lyrics of some of the songs on the White Album are a not particularly subtle call to violent overthrow of the establishment, whether or not the Beatles themselves took them seriously. They were not alone in this, of course. Violent revolution in one form or another was a constant theme in mid-to-late-sixties rock, standing unabashedly next to all the songs about peace and love.

Charlie didn't invent the counterculture's infatuation with madness as a separate, sometimes preferable reality, either; nor did he create the search for at least some of the tamer symptoms of that madness through the use of mind-bending drugs. Though Charlie may never have heard of him, R. D. Laing's *Politics of Experience* was a best-seller on college campuses, and whatever the Scottish psychiatrist's bizarre theories of sanity and insanity may have meant to him, when they trickled down to the mass youth culture — in books like *One Flew Over the Cuckoo's Nest* and films like *King of Hearts* and *Harold and Maude*, all of them with cult followings in the counterculture — what the kids read was: "Crazy is groovy!"

Charlie didn't even manage to dream up the Family lifestyle. There were communes and group marriages all across the country in the late sixties, and Robert Heinlein's *Stranger in a Strange Land*, a campus best-seller, featured an extraterrestrial traveler who built up a family that thought as one through group sex and mind reading ("grokking"). Michael Valentine Smith, the "stranger" of the title, is treated in the book as a hero, not a monster. I don't think it was an accident that Mary's baby, the first child born to Charlie by one of the Family women, was named Michael Valentine Manson.

Even the establishment he rejected was not totally disconnected from Charlie's warped truth. At the same time some of Charlie's Family was on trial, an army lieutenant named Calley was being defended by much of the right-wing establishment for "just obeying orders" in the killing of dozens of women and children in Vietnam. If a respected military commander could explain, "We had to destroy the village in order to save it," why shouldn't Charlie announce that "death is life"? The two statements are basically the same; only the victims were different.

I don't say any of this to exonerate Charlie or the rest of us. I only want to place our terrible crimes in their proper context: a world that worships death and sin instead of turning to life and light. Charlie, like others before him, just broke down the facades and let the vile, demonic truth run loose for all to see. But God and His love is greater than Charlie's madness or the world's madness disguised as the way things are. And one day God's Kingdom, not Helter Skelter, will come down, and it will be the City of God, the New Jerusalem where the Creator lives in the midst of His Creation, and all evil — personal and corporate, seen and unseen — will be healed.

Until then, the only sane way to live is in the hope of that healing that is to come. In this present world of darkness and death, the only way to truly live is in Christ, because He is the only true life there is, the only light.

My parents have come to the Men's Colony twice since my conversion, and both times we have filled the visitors' trailer we're assigned with praise and thanksgiving to God for finally bringing us back together again in Him after so much grief and pain. The scars are there, but scars mean healing. And my parents, through the anguish of it all, have themselves come to a deeper, more Spirit-filled experience of the faith they always held. It's as King David sang in one of his Psalms:

> *Weeping may tarry for the night, but joy comes with the morning . . . Thou hast turned for me my mourning into dancing . . . That my soul may praise thee and not be silent. O Lord my God, I will give thanks to thee forever. Psalms 30:5, 11, 12 RSV*

My deepest prayer is that these words could become true for all those who have suffered so much because of me. I pray it each day. I pray it now.

CPSIA information can be obtained
at www.ICGtesting.com
Printed in the USA
LVHW090117230521
688250LV00004B/209